hamlyn

Chocolate

Joanna Farrow

Note

Both metric and imperial measurements have been given in all recipes.
Use one set of measurements only, and not a mixture of both.

Standard level spoon measurements are used in all recipes.
1 tablespoon = one 15 ml spoon
1 teaspoon = one 5 ml spoon

The Department of Health advises that eggs should not be consumed raw.
This book contains dishes made with raw or lightly cooked eggs. It is
prudent for vulnerable people such as pregnant and nursing mothers,
invalids, the elderly, babies and young children to avoid uncooked or lightly
cooked dishes made with eggs. Once prepared, these dishes should be kept
refrigerated and used promptly.

This book includes dishes made with nuts and nut derivatives. It is advisable
for customers with known allergic reactions to nuts and nut derivatives and
those who may be potentially vulnerable to these allergies, such as pregnant
and nursing mothers, invalids, the elderly, babies and children to avoid
dishes made with nuts and nut oils. It is also prudent to check the labels of
pre-prepared ingredients for the possible inclusion of nut derivatives.

Ovens should be pre-heated to the specified temperature – if using a fan-
assisted oven, follow the manufacturer's instructions for adjusting the time
and the temperature.

First published in Great Britain in 2005 by Hamlyn,
a division of Octopus Publishing Group Ltd
2–4 Heron Quays, London E14 4JP

ISBN 0 600 61218 X
EAN 9780600612186

A CIP catalogue record for this book is available
from the British Library.

Printed and bound in China

10 9 8 7 6 5 4 3 2 1

Contents

Introduction
Chocolate is one of our favourite foods, whether it is comfortingly baked in a rich pudding, lavishly swirled into a creamy dessert or simply snapped from a bar. We're becoming increasingly discerning about the quality of chocolate available and are more willing to experiment as we get to grips with chocolate's incredible versatility.

About chocolate

Chocolate comes from the cocoa tree, which grows in humid, tropical regions around the equator. The large cocoa beans are harvested and left to ferment before being dried and shipped abroad. Fermenting is an important part of the production process because this is when the flavour develops, and cocoa beans that are fully fermented produce the best quality chocolate. After roasting, the beans undergo various treatments to produce cocoa solids, which are the basic ingredient of all chocolate products, and it's the production process that determines the quality of the chocolate. When you buy plain or milk chocolate, remember that the higher the proportion of cocoa solids, the purer the chocolate flavour will be.

Types of chocolate

There's an increasingly extensive range of chocolate available for both cooking and eating. The darkest **plain chocolate** contains 80 per cent or more cocoa solids and has an intensely chocolaty (though not necessarily bitter) flavour because of its lower sugar content. Perfect for those who prefer a less sweet, richer flavour, it's also the best for use in savoury chocolate recipes. Slightly sweeter is plain chocolate that contains 60–70 per cent cocoa solids. This has a dense chocolaty flavour and is a good 'all-rounder', ideal for recipes in this book that are made with plain chocolate. It melts well to a smooth, glossy texture and retains its full flavour. Less expensive brands

of plain chocolate contain 30–40 per cent cocoa solids. These are acceptable in family puddings and cakes, but you might like to splash out on the purer chocolate for special occasions.

Milk chocolate is considerably sweeter than plain chocolate and has added milk, sugar and flavourings, such as vanilla. It contains 20–30 per cent cocoa solids. Again, use the percentage of cocoa solids as a guide when you are buying.

White chocolate contains no solids. Instead, it is made with cocoa butter (the edible fat that is extracted from the beans during processing) and milk, sugar and flavouring.

Cocoa powder, a by-product of the processing method, has a strong, bitter flavour. Good for intensifying the flavour of chocolate, it should always be cooked and needs additional sweetening.

Never use chocolate-flavoured cake covering, which is usually sold alongside baking products in supermarkets. It's an imitation chocolate-flavoured bar of sugar, vegetable oils and flavourings.

Working with chocolate

Much of the success in chocolate cookery results from a knowledge of its unique qualities when melted or shaped, particularly for decorative cakes and desserts.

Melting chocolate

On the hob

Break the chocolate into pieces and put them in a heatproof bowl. Rest the bowl over a pan of very gently simmering water, making sure that the base of the bowl doesn't come in contact with the water. Once the chocolate starts to melt, turn off the heat and leave it until it is completely melted, stirring once or twice until no lumps remain. It's crucial that no water gets into the bowl while the chocolate is melting – steam from the pan, for example – because this will make the melted chocolate solidify. When you are pouring the melted chocolate on to paper for making chocolate decorations, wipe the base of the bowl with a cloth as soon as you take it from the heat, so that no condensed steam drips into the chocolate.

In the microwave

Use a microwave-proof bowl and melt the chocolate on medium power in one-minute spurts, checking frequently.

In the oven

Put the chocolate in a small ovenproof bowl or dish and leave the bowl in a low oven, 110°C (225°F), Gas Mark ¼, checking frequently. Alternatively, put it in an oven that's been switched off after being used for baking.

With other ingredients

Butter, cream, milk, liqueur or water can be melted with chocolate (see individual recipes). Because of the high fat or sugar content of butter and liqueur, note that the melting time will be reduced.

Tempering chocolate

The technique of heating and cooling chocolate before use is known as tempering. It's not essential for any of the recipes in this book and certainly not necessary when you are adding chocolate to cakes and bakes. It does, however, give a glossy finish and better texture to chocolate that's used for moulded shapes – the mousse cases on page 64, for example – or for decorations and confectionery. It also prolongs the keeping quality of chocolate sweets and reduces the risk of discoloration or 'bloom' dulling the surface. Chocolatiers temper chocolate to precise temperatures using a thermometer and working on a marble slab with a scraper. This in an easier, quicker way.

To temper chocolate

Break the chocolate into pieces and melt over a pan of simmering water (see above). Remove the bowl from the heat and leave to cool. This will take at least 30 minutes. Stir the melted chocolate gently and frequently as it cools, until it starts to thicken. Return the bowl to the heat and reheat the chocolate very gently so that it thins down but doesn't completely melt. You can use the tempered chocolate now or leave it over the heat until you're ready.

Using chocolate

Chocolate can be grated, curled, scribbled or melted and modelled into almost any shape. Some techniques take a matter of minutes, while other more imaginative, sculptural forms – the chocolate cases on page 68, for example – require a little more patience and planning. Once made, chocolate decorations keep well in a cool place for up to a week. For special cakes and desserts, you might prefer to temper the chocolate first.

Grated chocolate

Scatter some coarsely grated plain, milk or white chocolate over creamy desserts, ice creams and chilled drinks to make them look really appealing. If the chocolate bar is difficult to grate and breaks into tiny, brittle specks, warm it, very briefly, in the microwave first to soften it.

Chocolate curls

Use a potato peeler to pare off thick curls of chocolate from a bar and scatter them over cheesecakes, ice cream, trifles, cakes and chocolate mousses. The chunkier the chocolate bar, the larger the curls will be. Again, soften the bar, very briefly, in the microwave before use if it's too brittle.

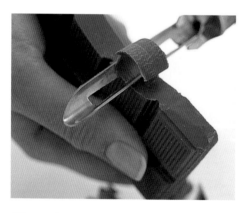

Chocolate caraque

These professional-looking curls take a little more effort but are well worth making for a special cake or dessert. They'll keep well in the refrigerator for several weeks, or in the freezer for longer.

Spread melted chocolate in a thin layer on a marble slab or a clean, smooth surface, such as a new, plastic chopping board or sturdy baking sheet. Leave to set. Holding a knife at an angle, draw it across the chocolate so that you scrape off curls. If the chocolate is too soft and doesn't curl, pop it in the refrigerator for a few minutes. If it is brittle and breaks off in thin shards, leave it at room temperature for a while before trying again.

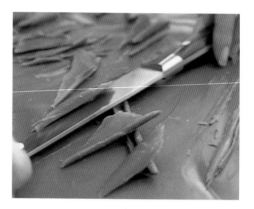

Chocolate shavings

To make more elaborate curls for special cakes and desserts melt 300 g (10 oz) plain or white chocolate with 25 g (1 oz) unsalted butter. Turn the mixture into a clean 250 g (8 oz) butter or margarine tub and leave until set but not brittle. Remove from the tub and pare off shavings. Protect the end of the slab with foil to prevent the heat of your hand melting the chocolate.

Chocolate scribbles

Line a tray with nonstick baking paper. Fill a paper piping bag with a little melted chocolate and snip off the merest tip. 'Draw' shapes on the paper – scribbled lines, curvy swirls or filigree patterns – and leave them to set. Peel the paper away from the scribbles and use them to decorate chilled desserts. Don't make the patterns too delicate or they will break.

Chocolate-dipped fruits

This is a great serving idea for summer fruits, such as strawberries and cherries, or for physalis, banana chunks and dates. Half-dip the fruit into melted chocolate, let the excess drip off and place the fruit on a sheet of nonstick baking paper until set. This technique can also be used for covering chocolate fudge, truffles or nuts.

Chocolate leaves

Firm but flexible leaves, such as fresh bay or rose, are best for making decorations for festive desserts and chocolate logs. Thoroughly wash and dry the leaves and brush or spoon a little chocolate on to the underside. Leave to set, then gently peel away the leaves.

Chocolate ribbons

Cut out 15 x 3 cm (6 x 1¼ inch) strips of nonstick baking paper. Spread melted chocolate over the strips, taking it almost to the edges. Arrange about 6 small wooden spoons, pens or chunky pencils in a row and spaced slightly apart on a small tray. Lift the chocolate strips over them so that they set in ribbony waves. Leave to set, then carefully peel away the paper.

Jagged chocolate brittle

Spread melted chocolate on a tray or baking sheet lined with nonstick baking paper. If you like, scatter some finely chopped toasted nuts over the chocolate, chill until really brittle, then peel away the paper and snap the chocolate into jagged shards. Spear into chocolate desserts and special-occasion cakes.

Cut-outs

Use small biscuit or cake cutters (available from specialist shops) to make shapes for decorating cakes and desserts. Spread melted chocolate on a tray lined with nonstick baking paper. Leave it to set, then press out the shapes with the cutters. These are good decorations for younger children to experiment with.

Equipment *You will need very little special equipment to cook with chocolate, and you will probably already have most of the basic items – large and small heavy-based saucepans, hand mixers, whisks, knives and brushes. If you are going to make a lot of recipes with chocolate, you will find the following items especially useful.*

Bowls

You can never have too many bowls. Some recipes, particularly desserts, require several, and you won't want to keep stopping to wash up. Chocolate is usually melted in a small, preferably heatproof glass, bowl that fits snugly over a saucepan. Remember that you don't want the bowl to sink so far into the pan that its base touches the water, but nor do you want it to be so big that it's balanced precariously on top of the pan. In most of the recipes in this book, the melted chocolate is added to other ingredients, so a small bowl will

suffice. When other ingredients are added to the melted chocolate, the recipe will specify a larger bowl so that you do not have to transfer the ingredients between bowls unnecessarily. Use a larger pan for the water on these occasions.

Palette knives

These are essential tools for achieving a smooth, even coverage of icing or ganache. You'll need both large and small knives, depending on the size of the cake. They are also useful for spreading melted chocolate thinly on paper to make decorations.

Cool surface

A marble slab is the best surface for setting chocolate caraque and other chocolate decorations. A small one that's not too heavy is ideal, because you can put it in the refrigerator to speed up setting. If you haven't got a marble slab but need another firm surface you can put in the refrigerator so that decorations can firm up, use a thoroughly clean wooden chopping board (preferably one kept for fruit and sweet dishes) or a thick plate or glass board or tray.

Dipping fork

Use a long, thin-pronged fork for dipping fruits and sweets into chocolate so that the chocolate doesn't clog up the tines but drips back into the bowl.

Metal moulds

Small metal moulds are perfect for individual portions of puddings and desserts and are used in several recipes in this book. Traditional 'pudding-shaped' moulds have a capacity of 150 ml (¼ pint), and the slightly smaller, straight-sided dariole moulds have a capacity of 125 ml (4 fl oz). The two are interchangeable in recipes, but bear in mind that rich chocolate desserts are often better in smaller moulds.

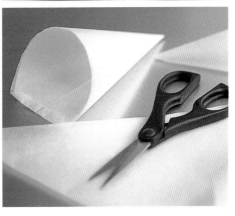

Paper piping bags

Paper bags are perfect for piping scribbled decorations directly on cakes and desserts or on paper for setting. Unlike cloth bags, paper ones are disposable and save you the trouble of washing them. To make a paper piping bag, cut out a 25 cm (10 inch) square of greaseproof paper or nonstick baking paper and fold it diagonally in half to make a triangle. Cut along the folded line. Holding the centre of the long edge towards you, curl the right-hand point of the triangle over to meet the centre point, forming a cone. Bring the left-hand point over the cone so that the three points meet. Fold the paper over several times at the points to stop the paper unravelling. Half-fill the bag with melted chocolate and fold down the open end to secure the bag before snipping off the tip. Test the flow and snip off a little more for a thicker flow. If the chocolate sets in the bag before you've had a chance to use it, pop it briefly into the microwave until softened. If you don't want to make or use a paper piping bag, effective finishes can still be made over cakes and desserts by drizzling melted chocolate back and forth from a teaspoon.

Basic recipes *These are the recipes that crop up several times in the book, such as a crisp, sweet biscuity pastry, or those that make fabulous accompaniments to puddings and desserts. Choose the Glossy Chocolate Sauce for a really rich topping or opt for the Chocolate Orange Sabayon if you prefer a lighter alternative.*

Glossy chocolate syrup *Some puddings and desserts need a lighter alternative to a sauce. This smooth chocolate syrup adds plenty of flavour and can be used for an informal yet decorative presentation.*

PREPARATION TIME: 2 minutes

COOKING TIME: 3 minutes

SERVES 6–8

25 g (1 oz) caster sugar
150 ml (¼ pint) water
50 g (2 oz) plain chocolate, chopped

1 Put the sugar in a small heavy-based saucepan with the water and heat gently, stirring until the sugar dissolves. Bring to the boil and boil for 1 minute.

2 Remove from the heat and stir in the chocolate. Leave until melted, then reheat gently until the syrup is smooth and glossy. Turn the syrup into a small jug, ready for pouring.

Variations

For a spiced syrup, add ½ teaspoon ground cinnamon to the pan when dissolving the sugar. For a coffee syrup, add 1 teaspoon espresso granules with the chocolate. For a liqueur syrup, add a splash of brandy, orange or coffee liqueur.

Glossy chocolate sauce

Almost everyone loves a good chocolate sauce, the darker and glossier the better. Serve it with hot chocolate puddings or spooned generously over vanilla ice cream.

PREPARATION TIME: 5 minutes

COOKING TIME: 3 minutes

SERVES 6

125 g (4 oz) caster sugar

125 ml (4 fl oz) water

200 g (7 oz) plain chocolate, chopped

25 g (1 oz) unsalted butter

1 Put the sugar in a small heavy-based saucepan with the water. Cook over a low heat, stirring constantly with a wooden spoon until the sugar has completely dissolved.

2 Bring to the boil and boil for 1 minute, then leave to cool for a further minute. Add the chocolate and butter and leave until both have melted.

3 Stir until smooth and glossy, returning to a gentle heat if the last of the chocolate doesn't melt completely.

Cook's tip

If it's made in advance, chocolate sauce will solidify. Reheat very gently so that the chocolate doesn't spoil.

Chocolate fudge icing
The muscovado syrup gives this icing a real depth of flavour. Use it to sandwich and spread over the top of a chocolate sponge or to cover chocolate muffins.

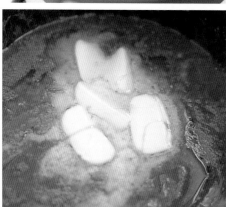

PREPARATION TIME: 10 minutes

COOKING TIME: 10 minutes

SERVES sufficient to sandwich and cover the top of an 18–20 cm (7–8 inch) cake

150 g (5 oz) plain chocolate, chopped
150 ml (¼ pint) double cream
125 g (4 oz) light muscovado sugar
65 g (2½ oz) unsalted butter
1 teaspoon vanilla extract

1 Melt the chocolate in a small bowl. Put the cream and sugar in a medium-sized heavy-based saucepan and stir gently until the sugar has dissolved.

2 Bring the cream mixture to the boil and simmer, without stirring, for about 4 minutes until it is bubbling vigorously and has become thickened and caramely.

3 Remove the mixture from the heat and stir in the butter until it has melted.

4 Add the melted chocolate and vanilla extract and turn the icing into a bowl. Cool, then chill for about 30 minutes until it is thickened and spreadable.

Cook's tip
If it is chilled for several hours, the icing will solidify. If this happens, leave it at room temperature for a while or soften carefully in the microwave.

Chocolate orange sabayon *This light and*

airy sauce is lovely with poached fruits or hot or cold chocolate puddings, which would be overpowered by a more substantial sauce.

PREPARATION TIME: 3 minutes

COOKING TIME: 5–10 minutes

SERVES 4

50 g (2 oz) white chocolate, broken up

**finely grated rind of 1 orange, plus
    4 tablespoons juice**

1 tablespoon lemon juice

4 egg yolks

1 Put the chocolate, orange rind and juice and lemon juice in a large heatproof bowl over a pan of gently simmering water, making sure the base of the bowl does not come into contact with the water. Allow the ingredients to melt before adding the yolks.

2 Use a hand-held electric whisk or balloon whisk to beat the ingredients for 5–10 minutes until the mixture is light and aerated.

3 Use immediately or leave the sauce to stand over the pan, covered with a lid and with the heat turned off, for up to 30 minutes.

Chocolate crème anglaise

Like homemade vanilla-flavoured crème anglaise, this custard can be both comforting and rather special. Try it spooned over chocolate puddings and pastries.

PREPARATION TIME: 10 minutes

COOKING TIME: 15 minutes

SERVES 6

300 ml (½ pint) milk

300 ml (½ pint) single cream

6 egg yolks

25 g (1 oz) caster sugar

1 teaspoon cornflour

75 g (3 oz) plain chocolate, chopped

1 Put the milk and cream in a medium-sized heavy-based saucepan and bring the mixture slowly to the boil. In a large bowl whisk together the egg yolks, sugar and cornflour.

2 Pour the hot milk and cream over the yolks mixture, whisking well. Return to a clean pan.

3 Cook the custard over a gentle heat, stirring constantly with a wooden spoon for about 10 minutes until it thickly coats the back of the spoon. Do not let the custard boil or it might curdle.

4 Remove the custard from the heat and stir in the chocolate until melted. Serve warm with the pudding of your choice.

Variation

For white chocolate custard, use 100 g (3½ oz) chopped white chocolate instead of plain and omit the sugar.

Rich chocolate ganache

Chocolate ganache sounds rather exotic, but it is simply a blend of chocolate and cream, which is easy to make and one of the most useful components of chocolate baking. Use it as a cake filling or topping or as a basic mixture for chocolate truffles.

PREPARATION TIME: 5 minutes, plus cooling

COOKING TIME: 3 minutes

SERVES sufficient to cover a 20 cm (8 inch) chocolate cake

300 ml (½ pint) double cream
300 g (10 oz) plain chocolate, chopped

1 Heat the cream in a medium-sized heavy-based saucepan until it is bubbling around the edges. Remove from the heat and add the chocolate.

2 Leave to stand for a few minutes until the chocolate has melted, then stir well and turn the mixture into a bowl.

3 Chill until the mixture holds its shape when stirred – roughly 15–45 minutes.

White chocolate ganache

White chocolate is more temperamental to cook with than plain, so the technique for making ganache is slightly different. Once made, use it in exactly the same way.

PREPARATION TIME: 5 minutes, plus chilling

COOKING TIME: 3 minutes

MAKES sufficient to cover a 20 cm (8 inch) chocolate cake

300 ml (½ pint) double cream

300 g (10 oz) white chocolate, chopped

1 Put half the cream in a medium-sized heavy-based saucepan and heat gently until it is bubbling around the edges. Remove from the heat and stir in the chopped chocolate.

2 Leave to stand for a few minutes until the chocolate has melted, then stir lightly and turn into a bowl. Chill for about 15 minutes until cool.

3 Add the remaining cream to the bowl and whisk with a hand-held electric mixer until the ganache just starts to hold its shape. Don't over-whisk or it will start to separate.

Crisp chocolate pastry
Dark, crisp and buttery, this dessert pastry is more like a sweet biscuit paste and is perfect for chocolate tarts and pies. Roll it out as thinly as possible.

PREPARATION TIME: 10 minutes

MAKES sufficient to line a 20–23 cm (8–9 inch) pastry case

15 g (½ oz) cocoa powder

125 g (4 oz) plain flour

25 g (1 oz) icing sugar

75 g (3 oz) lightly salted butter, diced

1 egg yolk

1 Sift the cocoa powder, flour and icing sugar into a bowl. Add the butter and rub in with the fingertips until the mixture resembles fine breadcrumbs.

2 Add the egg yolk and 1 teaspoon cold water and mix to a dough. Alternatively, blend the butter into the flour mixture in a food processor, then blend in the egg yolk and water until the mixture binds together.

3 Turn the dough on to a lightly floured surface and knead lightly until smooth. Wrap and chill for at least 30 minutes before using.

4 Put a greased flan ring or tin on a baking sheet. Roll out the pastry so that it is about 5 cm (2 inches) larger all round than the diameter of the ring or tin. Roll the pastry loosely around the rolling pin and lift it over the tin. Carefully unroll it into the tin, gently easing it into the tin and taking care not to stretch it or leave air gaps underneath. Carefully press the pastry into the flutes with your fingers. Turn any surplus pastry outwards from the rim, then roll the rolling pin straight over the top so that the surplus pastry is cut and falls away, leaving a neat edge.

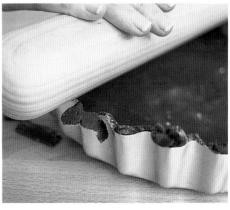

Savoury chocolate *Despite the fact that most of us think of chocolate in relation only to sweet recipes, its use in savoury dishes is well established in some parts of the world. Used in very small quantities, a mere hint of chocolate thickens a sauce, adds body and gloss, and provides a subtle chocolaty flavour that complements rather than dominates the other flavours in the dish.*

If you haven't experimented with savoury chocolate before, the meaty recipes in this chapter make a good starting point, but don't use anything less than the most bitter (at least 80% cocoa solids) dark chocolate to achieve a full, rounded flavour. For special entertaining or a casual supper, these main-course dishes will certainly provide a talking point, but if you're not sure what the diners' responses will be, leave them to guess the secret ingredient.

Marinated duck with ginger sauce

Although distinctively chocolaty, this fabulous sauce has a fresh tang that's the perfect complement for the richness of the duck.

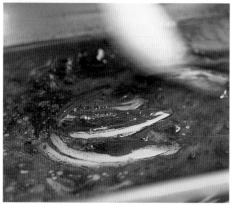

PREPARATION TIME: 20 minutes, plus marinating

COOKING TIME: 40 minutes

OVEN TEMPERATURE: 180°C (350°F), Gas Mark 4

SERVES 4

4 large duck breasts

1 onion, sliced

1 celery stick, chopped

4 tablespoons clear honey

50 g (2 oz) fresh root ginger, grated

3 tablespoons lemon juice

1 tablespoon soy sauce

2 teaspoons five spice powder

1 tablespoon groundnut oil

15 g (½ oz) plain chocolate, chopped

1 Score each piece of duck several times with a sharp knife. Scatter the onion and celery in a shallow dish and place the duck on top.

2 Mix together the honey, ginger, lemon juice, soy sauce and five spice powder and pour it over the duck. Cover and leave to marinate in the refrigerator for at least 6 hours or overnight, turning once.

3 Drain the duck and strain the marinade into a small bowl. Pat the duck dry on kitchen paper. Heat the oil in a heavy-based frying pan and fry the duck pieces, skin side down, for 5 minutes until dark golden. Transfer to a roasting tin and cook in a preheated oven, 180°C (350°F), Gas Mark 4, for about 30 minutes until tender. Transfer the duck to a warmed dish and drain off all the fat from the tin.

4 Add the reserved marinade to the tin and bring it to the boil. Reduce the heat and stir in the chocolate to make a smooth, glossy sauce. Spoon over the duck on warmed serving plates.

Marinated duck with ginger sauce

Italian sweet and sour chicken

A dish to suit almost any occasion, from family supper to entertaining friends, this is ideal with polenta, which can be used to mop up the sweet, tangy chocolate juices.

PREPARATION TIME: 20 minutes

COOKING TIME: 55 minutes

SERVES 4

3 tablespoons olive oil

1 onion, finely chopped

50 g (2 oz) lean smoked bacon, diced

2 teaspoons dark muscovado sugar

4 chicken thighs, skinned

4 chicken drumsticks, skinned

3 garlic cloves, crushed

2 bay leaves

75 ml (3 fl oz) red wine vinegar

300 ml (½ pint) chicken stock

50 g (2 oz) sultanas

40 g (1½ oz) plain chocolate, chopped

50 g (2 oz) pine nuts, lightly toasted

salt and pepper

1 Heat the oil in a large heavy-based saucepan and gently fry the onion and bacon for 5 minutes until golden. Add the sugar and chicken and fry for a further 5 minutes, turning the chicken frequently until it is golden.

2 Add the garlic, bay leaves, vinegar and stock and bring to the boil. Reduce the heat, cover with a lid and simmer very gently for 40 minutes or until the chicken is tender.

3 Drain the chicken and keep the pieces warm. Stir the sultanas, chocolate and half the pine nuts into the sauce and cook gently for 5 minutes. Season to taste. Arrange the chicken on serving plates and spoon over the sauce. Scatter over the remaining pine nuts and serve.

Mexican chicken mole

This spicy Mexican speciality is renowned for the subtle addition of chocolate in the spicy, nutty sauce. It is good party dish because quantities can easily be doubled up.

PREPARATION TIME: 20 minutes

COOKING TIME: 1 hour

OVEN TEMPERATURE: 190°C (375°F), Gas Mark 5

SERVES 4

2 tablespoons olive oil

1 oven-ready chicken, about 1.25 kg (2¾ lb)

1 large onion, quartered

4 garlic cloves, halved

600 ml (1 pint) water

1 tablespoon olive oil

1 onion, roughly chopped

1 red chilli, deseeded and roughly chopped

1 teaspoon cumin seeds

½ teaspoon ground cinnamon

¼ teaspoon ground cloves

40 g (1½ oz) blanched almonds

2 tablespoons sesame seeds

1 corn or wheat tortilla, about 40 g (1½ oz), torn into pieces

15 g (½ oz) plain chocolate, chopped

small handful fresh coriander leaves, chopped

salt

1 Heat the oil in a large flameproof casserole and fry the chicken on all sides until deep golden. Add the onion, garlic, water and a little salt, bring to the boil and cover with a lid. Bake in a preheated oven, 190°C (375°F), Gas Mark 5, for about 1 hour until cooked through.

2 Meanwhile, start the sauce. Heat the oil in a frying pan and fry the onion and chilli for 3 minutes, stirring. Add the spices and fry gently for a further 2 minutes.

3 Put the almonds, sesame seeds and tortilla into a food processor and blend until coarsely ground. Add the contents of the frying pan and blend to a smooth paste.

4 Transfer the chicken to a serving plate and keep warm. Measure 300 ml (½ pint) of the stock (reserving the remainder for another recipe) and add it to the processor. Blend until smooth and pour the sauce back into the frying pan.

5 Stir in the chocolate and a little of the coriander and heat gently until the chocolate has melted. Carve the chicken and serve with the sauce, with the remaining coriander sprinkled over.

Lambs' liver with balsamic glaze

Smooth and glossy, the sweet tangy sauce is a great accompaniment to the firm texture of the liver and crisp, salty bacon.

PREPARATION TIME: 5 minutes

COOKING TIME: 10 minutes

SERVES 4

625 g (1¼ lb) lambs' liver, thinly sliced

150 g (5 oz) thin cut back bacon

25 g (1 oz) butter

1 tablespoon olive oil

3 tablespoons balsamic vinegar

15 g (½ oz) plain chocolate, chopped

salt and pepper

1 Pat the liver dry on kitchen paper and season lightly with salt and pepper. Fry the bacon in a large heavy-based saucepan until crisp. Drain and keep warm.

2 Melt the butter with the oil in the pan and fry the liver for about 2 minutes on each side until golden-brown. Drain and keep warm.

3 Add the vinegar and chocolate to the pan and cook gently, stirring until the chocolate has melted, to make a smooth, glossy sauce. Spoon the sauce over the liver and bacon on warmed serving plates.

Braised lamb shanks with vegetables

Allow at least a day, or preferably two, to marinate the meat so that it has plenty of time to become tenderized and to absorb all the marinade flavours.

PREPARATION TIME: 25 minutes, plus marinating

COOKING TIME: 2 hours

OVEN TEMPERATURE: 160°C (325°F), Gas Mark 3

SERVES 6

6 lamb shanks

2 onions

8 thyme sprigs

2 bay leaves

2 teaspoons cocoa powder

450 ml (¾ pint) red wine

3 garlic cloves

1 teaspoon black peppercorns

4 tablespoons olive oil

200 g (7 oz) baby carrots

150 g (5 oz) broad beans

6 pickled walnuts, halved

25 g (1 oz) plain chocolate, chopped

parsley, to garnish

salt

1 Put the lamb shanks in a large, shallow container in which they fit quite snugly. Roughly chop one of the onions and put in a blender or food processor with the herbs, cocoa powder, wine, garlic and peppercorns. Blend until slightly pulpy and pour over the lamb. Cover and leave to marinate for 24–48 hours, turning the meat several times.

2 Drain the lamb, reserving the marinade, and pat the meat dry on kitchen paper. Heat the oil in a large frying pan and fry the lamb for about 10 minutes, turning frequently until deep golden. Transfer the meat to a shallow ovenproof dish or roasting tin.

3 Finely chop the remaining onion and fry in the pan for 3 minutes. Strain the marinade into the pan and bring to the boil. Pour it over the lamb and cover the dish with a lid or foil. Cook in a preheated oven, 160°C (325°F), Gas Mark 3, for 1½ hours or until the lamb is tender.

4 Scatter the carrots, beans and pickled walnuts around the lamb and return to the oven for a further 15 minutes or until the vegetables are tender.

5 Drain the meat and vegetables and transfer to serving plates. Stir the chocolate into the pan juices until melted. Check the seasoning and pour the sauce into a jug. Serve the lamb drizzled with the sauce and garnished with parsley.

Hot puddings *Hot chocolate puddings inevitably come at the top of the list of comfort dishes, whether they are in the form of a melting chocolate sauce under a sweet sugary crust, smooth airy soufflés, glossy fudge fondues or indulgent steamed puddings. Some of these puddings are quick and easy to assemble, making them perfect for family meals, while others take a little more time and are better suited to entertaining.*

To save last-minute preparation, some of these, such as the soufflés or crumble, can be made ahead, ready for last minute cooking. Others, such as the Syrupy Chocolate Tart or Chocolate, Rosemary and Pine Nut Tart, can be made well in advance and warmed through gently to serve. Topped with melting ice cream, homemade custard or pouring cream, chocolate puddings are the ultimate indulgence.

Chocolate nut crumble

A perfect pudding for winter comfort. For total indulgence, serve it topped with melting vanilla ice cream or lashings of chocolate custard.

PREPARATION TIME: 20 minutes

COOKING TIME: 40 minutes

OVEN TEMPERATURE: 190°C (375°F), Gas Mark 5

SERVES 4–5

175 g (6 oz) plain flour

125 g (4 oz) unsalted butter, diced

175 g (6 oz) demerara sugar

875 g (1¾ lb) cooking apples

40 g (1½ oz) fresh root ginger

150 g (5 oz) plain chocolate, broken up

25 g (1 oz) hazelnuts, roughly chopped

1 Put the flour and butter in a food processor and blend until the mixture starts to resemble coarse breadcrumbs. Add 100 g (3½ oz) of the sugar and blend until evenly mixed.

2 Peel, core and slice the apples and scatter them in a shallow 1.5 litre (2½ pint) ovenproof dish. Sprinkle over the remaining sugar. Finely chop the ginger and toss with the sugared apples. Scatter the chocolate over the mixture and push some pieces down into the fruit.

3 Sprinkle the crumble mixture over the apple mixture and scatter over the hazelnuts. Bake in a preheated oven, 190°C (375°F), Gas Mark 5, for about 40 minutes or until turning golden. Leave to stand for 10 minutes before serving.

Hot chocolate and brandied prune soufflés

These intensely chocolaty soufflés can be prepared several hours in advance, leaving you free to enjoy your meal.

PREPARATION TIME: 15 minutes

COOKING TIME: 15 minutes

OVEN TEMPERATURE: 200°C (400°F), Gas Mark 6

SERVES 8

butter, for greasing

25 g (1 oz) caster sugar, plus extra for dusting

200 g (7 oz) no-soak prunes, halved

½ teaspoon cornflour

6 tablespoons brandy

150 g (5 oz) plain chocolate, broken up

3 tablespoons double cream

6 eggs, separated

cocoa powder, for dusting

1 Butter 8 150 ml (¼ pint) ramekin dishes or other small ovenproof serving dishes and dust each lightly with caster sugar. Put the prunes in a small saucepan with 125 ml (4 fl oz) water and simmer gently for 1 minute. Blend the cornflour with 1 tablespoon water and add to the pan. Cook, stirring over a gentle heat, for 1 minute or until the sauce has thickened. Stir in the brandy and divide the mixture among the dishes.

2 Melt the chocolate with the cream in a small bowl. Whisk the egg yolks with the sugar until thickened and pale. Stir in the chocolate cream.

3 Whisk the egg whites in a clean bowl until stiff. Use a large metal spoon to fold about a quarter of the whites into the chocolate mixture to lighten it, then fold in the remainder.

4 Spoon the mixture into the dishes and put them on a baking sheet. (If you are making them in advance, put them on a baking sheet and chill until ready to cook.) Bake in a preheated oven, 200°C (400°F), Gas Mark 6, for about 15 minutes until well risen and slightly springy. Dust with cocoa powder and serve immediately.

Chocolate fudge fondue *This smooth, glossy chocolate sauce is best served in little cups, surrounded by an assortment of flavour-contrasting dippers.*

PREPARATION TIME: 15 minutes

COOKING TIME: 10 minutes

SERVES 6

150 g (5 oz) light muscovado sugar
50 g (2 oz) unsalted butter
200 g (7 oz) plain chocolate, chopped
1 teaspoon vanilla extract
100 ml (3½ fl oz) soured cream
2 bananas
200 g (7 oz) sweet raisin bread
handful of strawberries and cherries

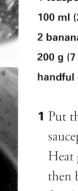

1 Put the sugar in a small heavy-based saucepan with 100 ml (3½ fl oz) water. Heat gently until the sugar dissolves, then bring to the boil and boil rapidly for about 4 minutes until the syrup is bubbling vigorously and looks dark and treacly.

2 Remove the saucepan from the heat and immerse the base in cold water to prevent further cooking. Add 2 tablespoons water, taking care because the syrup is likely to splutter. Return the saucepan to the heat and cook, stirring, until the syrup is smooth and glossy.

3 Add the butter, chocolate and vanilla extract and leave until melted, stirring frequently until the mixture is completely smooth. Stir in the cream and leave to stand while you prepare the dippers.

4 Cut the bananas diagonally into chunky pieces. Cut the bread into small, bite-sized chunks. Reheat the sauce until it is warm but not piping hot and pour into small serving cups. Arrange the fruit and bread around the cups to serve.

Marbled chocolate ginger pudding *An indulgent treat for anyone who can't resist steamed puddings. Marbling dark and light chocolate together provides everyone's favourite flavour.*

PREPARATION TIME: 25 minutes

COOKING TIME: 2¼ hours

SERVES 6

175 g (6 oz) plain chocolate

175 g (6 oz) white chocolate

175 g (6 oz) unsalted butter, softened

150 g (5 oz) caster sugar

3 eggs, beaten

175 g (6 oz) self-raising flour

50 g (2 oz) fresh root ginger, grated

1 quantity White Chocolate Custard, to serve
   (see page 14, variation)

1 Grease a 1.5 litre (2½ pint) pudding basin and line the base with a circle of greaseproof paper. Chop 50 g (2 oz) of each chocolate, keeping them separate. Melt the remaining plain and white chocolate in separate bowls.

2 Use an electric whisk to beat together the butter and sugar until pale and creamy. Gradually beat in the eggs, adding a little of the flour, if necessary, to prevent curdling. Stir in the remaining flour.

3 Transfer half the mixture to another bowl. Stir the melted and chopped plain chocolate and the ginger into one bowl and the chopped and melted white chocolate into the other. Place alternate spoonfuls of the 2 mixtures into the basin. Level the surface, then lightly swirl the mixtures together with a knife to create a marbled effect.

4 Cover the pudding with a double thickness of greaseproof paper, securing it under the rim with string. Cover with foil, crumpling it firmly under the rim. Put in a large saucepan and pour in boiling water to come halfway up the sides of the basin. Cover with a lid and steam for 2¼ hours, topping up with boiling water if necessary.

5 Invert the pudding on to a serving plate and serve in wedges with the custard.

White chocolate brioche pudding
Once you've tasted this fabulous pudding, you won't want to go back to it's culinary roots – a traditional bread and butter pudding.

PREPARATION TIME: 15 minutes, plus soaking

COOKING TIME: 30 minutes

OVEN TEMPERATURE: 190°C (375°), Gas Mark 5

SERVES 6

butter, for greasing

250 g (8 oz) white chocolate, broken up

25 g (1 oz) unsalted butter

250 g (8 oz) brioche, sliced

250 g (8 oz) fresh or frozen raspberries

4 eggs

600 ml (1 pint) milk

25 g (1 oz) caster sugar

icing sugar, for dusting

1 Butter the sides of a shallow 2 litre (3½ pint) ovenproof dish. Melt the chocolate with the butter in a small bowl. If the brioche came from a large loaf, cut the slices into smaller triangles or squares. Lay half the bread slices in the dish and spoon over half the chocolate sauce. Scatter with half the raspberries.

2 Lay the rest of the bread over the top and dot with the remaining sauce and raspberries. Beat together the eggs, milk and sugar and pour the mixture over the pudding. Leave to soak for 20 minutes.

3 Bake in a preheated oven, 190°C (375°F), Gas Mark 5, for about 30 minutes until the surface is turning pale golden and the custard is very lightly set. Leave to stand for 10 minutes, then serve dusted with icing sugar.

Variation
For a festive alternative, you can use the same quantity of Italian panettone instead of brioche.

Hot chocolate and Kahlua risotto

Chocolate risottos are smooth, creamy and comforting but chic enough for a casual dinner party if served in small cappuccino cups.

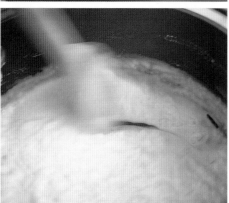

PREPARATION TIME: 10 minutes

COOKING TIME: 15 minutes

SERVES 4

450 ml (¾ pint) milk
15 g (½ oz) caster sugar
125 g (4 oz) risotto rice
4 tablespoons Kahlua or other coffee liqueur
150 g (5 oz) plain chocolate, roughly chopped
15 g (½ oz) chocolate coffee beans, crushed
crème fraîche, to serve

1 Put the milk in a large heavy-based saucepan with the sugar and heat until it is almost beginning to boil. Sprinkle in the rice, stirring, then reduce the heat to a very gentle simmer.

2 Cook the risotto gently for about 15 minutes, stirring frequently, until it is creamy and the rice has softened but still retains a nutty texture. (If the risotto becomes dry before the rice is cooked, add a splash more milk.)

3 Stir in the liqueur and half the chocolate and stir until the chocolate has melted. Quickly stir in the remaining chocolate and ladle into small, warmed bowls or coffee cups. Scatter with the coffee beans and serve with crème fraîche for swirling into the risotto.

Hot chocolate and Kahlua risotto

Chocolate, rosemary and pine nut tart

Fresh, aromatic herbs, such as rosemary, make delicious partners to chocolate in puddings and cakes.

PREPARATION TIME: 20 minutes

COOKING TIME: 45 minutes

OVEN TEMPERATURE: 200°C (400°F), Gas Mark 6, then 160°C (325°F), Gas Mark 3

SERVES 10–12

1 quantity Crisp Chocolate Pastry (see page 17)

375 g (12 oz) white chocolate

50 g (2 oz) unsalted butter

50 g (2 oz) caster sugar

3 eggs

1 tablespoon finely chopped rosemary

finely grated rind and juice of 1 lemon

125 g (4 oz) self-raising flour

75 g (3 oz) pine nuts

icing sugar, for dusting

1 Thinly roll out the pastry on a lightly floured surface and use it to line a 25 cm (10 inch) loose-based flan tin, 2.5 cm (1 inch) deep (see page 17). Line with greaseproof paper and baking beans and bake blind in a preheated oven, 200°C (400°F), Gas Mark 6, for 15 minutes. Remove the paper and beans and bake for a further 5 minutes. Reduce the oven temperature to 160°C (325°F), Gas Mark 3.

2 Chop 250 g (8 oz) of the chocolate. Break the remainder into pieces and melt it with the butter. Whisk together the sugar, eggs and rosemary in a large bowl. Stir in the melted chocolate mixture, lemon rind and juice and flour. Gently stir in all but 50 g (2 oz) of the chopped chocolate.

3 Turn the mixture into the pastry case. Scatter the pine nuts and remaining chocolate over the top. Bake for about 25 minutes until pale golden and just firm. Serve warm, dusted with icing sugar.

Syrupy chocolate tart

A cross between a pecan pie and a treacle tart, this recipe makes a heavenly treat. Serve with the Chocolate Orange Sabayon (see page 13) for plenty of tangy contrast.

PREPARATION TIME: 15 minutes

COOKING TIME: 50 minutes

OVEN TEMPERATURE: 200°C (400°F), Gas Mark 6, then 160°C (325°F), Gas Mark 3

SERVES 10

1 quantity Crisp Chocolate Pastry (see page 17)

150 g (5 oz) light muscovado sugar

250 ml (8 fl oz) maple syrup

100 g (3½ oz) unsalted butter

200 g (7 oz) plain chocolate, chopped

2 teaspoons vanilla extract

4 eggs, beaten

100 g (3½ oz) walnuts or pecans, roughly chopped

1 Thinly roll out the pastry on a lightly floured surface and use it to line a 23 cm (9 inch) loose-based flan tin, 4 cm (1½ inches) deep (see page 17). Line it with greaseproof paper and baking beans and bake blind in a preheated oven, 200°C (400°F), Gas Mark 6, for 15 minutes. Remove the paper and beans and bake for a further 5 minutes. Reduce the oven temperature to 160°C (325°F), Gas Mark 3.

2 Put the sugar, syrup and butter in a saucepan and heat gently until melted. Remove from the heat and add the chocolate, stirring until it has melted. Beat in the vanilla and eggs and turn the mixture into the pastry case.

3 Scatter the nuts over the top and bake the flan for 30 minutes or until the filling forms a cracked crust but still feels wobbly underneath. Leave to stand for 10 minutes before serving.

Chocolate fig tatin

Take a short cut to a delicious tarte tatin by using bought puff pastry, sandwiched with chocolaty layers. Serve warm topped with melting ice cream or crème fraîche.

PREPARATION TIME: 20 minutes

COOKING TIME: 35 minutes

OVEN TEMPERATURE: 200°C (400°F), Gas Mark 6

SERVES 6

100 g (3½ oz) plain chocolate, grated

1 teaspoon ground mixed spice

75 g (3 oz) caster sugar, plus 2 tablespoons

500 g (1 lb) puff pastry, thawed if frozen

75 g (3 oz) unsalted butter, plus extra for greasing

10 fresh figs, quartered

1 tablespoon lemon juice

vanilla ice cream or crème fraîche, to serve

1 Mix together the grated chocolate, spice and 2 tablespoons sugar. Cut the pastry into 3 evenly sized pieces and roll out each to a circle 25 cm (10 inches) across, using a plate or inverted bowl as a guide.

2 Scatter 2 rounds to within 2 cm (¾ inch) of the edges with the grated chocolate mixture. Stack the pastry layers so that the chocolate is sandwiched in 2 layers. Press the pastry down firmly around the edges.

3 Lightly butter the sides of a shallow 23 cm (9 inch) round baking tin, 4 cm (1½ inches) deep. (Don't use a loose-based tin.) Melt the butter in a frying pan. Add the sugar and heat gently until dissolved. Add the figs and cook for 3 minutes or until lightly coloured and the syrup begins to turn golden. Add the lemon juice.

4 Tip the figs into the tin, spreading them in an even layer. Lay the pastry over the figs, tucking the dough down inside the edges of the tin. Bake in a preheated oven, 200°C (400°F), Gas Mark 6, for 30 minutes until well risen and golden. Leave for 5 minutes, then loosen the edges and invert on to a serving plate.

Chocolate fig tatin

Heavenly chocolate pudding
This really is the ultimate hot chocolate pudding: an intensely chocolate-flavoured blend that's lightly baked so that a sugary crust forms over a smooth, creamy sauce.

PREPARATION TIME: 10 minutes

COOKING TIME: 10 minutes

OVEN TEMPERATURE: 160°C (325°F), Gas Mark 3

SERVES 4

100 g (3½ oz) milk chocolate, broken up

50 g (2 oz) unsalted butter

40 g (1½ oz) cocoa powder

75 g (3 oz) golden caster sugar

2 eggs, separated

1 teaspoon vanilla extract

4 tablespoons single cream

cocoa powder, for dusting

1 Melt the chocolate and butter in a large mixing bowl. Add the cocoa powder, 50 g (2 oz) of the sugar, the egg yolks, vanilla extract and cream, and beat the mixture to a smooth paste.

2 Whisk the egg whites in a clean bowl until peaking and gradually whisk in the remaining sugar. Use a large metal spoon to fold a quarter of the meringue into the chocolate mixture to lighten it, then fold in the remainder.

3 Divide the mixture between 4 small ramekin dishes or similar-sized ovenproof dishes. Bake in a preheated oven, 160°C (325°F), Gas Mark 3, for 8–10 minutes until a very thin crust has formed over the surface. Dust with cocoa powder and serve immediately.

Variation
For an alcoholic kick, stir 2 tablespoons brandy, rum or orange liqueur into the mixture at step 1.

Chocolate, pecan and maple crêpes *For maximum enjoyment, eat these lacy chocolate pancakes while their freshly cooked aroma still lingers.*

PREPARATION TIME: 20 minutes

COOKING TIME: 20 minutes

MAKES 8

100 g (3½ oz) plain flour

15 g (½ oz) cocoa powder

2 tablespoons caster sugar

1 egg

300 ml (½ pint) milk

a little oil, for frying

50 g (2 oz) pecan nuts, lightly toasted

175 ml (6 fl oz) maple syrup

8 scoops vanilla ice cream

1 quantity Glossy Chocolate Sauce
   (see page 11)

1 Sift the flour and cocoa powder into a bowl and stir in the sugar. Make a well in the centre and add the egg and a little of the milk. Whisk the egg with the milk, gradually incorporating the flour and the remaining milk to make a smooth batter. Pour into a jug.

2 Heat a little oil in a medium-sized crêpe pan or heavy-based frying pan until it is beginning to smoke. Drain off the excess oil and pour a little batter into the pan, tilting it so that the batter spreads in a thin layer. Cook gently until lightly browned on the underside. Flip over and cook the other side until it is browned. Slide the crêpe on to a warmed plate. Cook the remaining batter in the same way, lightly oiling the pan each time.

3 Roughly chop the nuts and mix them with the maple syrup.

4 Fold the crêpes into quarters on serving plates and spoon over the nut syrup. Top with scoops of ice cream and some chocolate sauce.

Roasted plums with ginger sauce

You can make this quick and easy pudding with almost any reasonably decent plums, because roasting in wine softens them and brings out their flavour.

PREPARATION TIME: 15 minutes

COOKING TIME: 15 minutes

OVEN TEMPERATURE: 220°C (425°F), Gas Mark 7

SERVES 6

625 g (1¼ lb) dessert plums

4 bay leaves

100 ml (3½ fl oz) white wine

2 tablespoons clear honey

50 g (2 oz) fresh root ginger

1 tablespoon caster sugar

75 ml (3 fl oz) water

150 g (5 oz) white chocolate, chopped

100 g (3½ oz) crème fraîche

1 Halve and stone the plums and arrange them in a single layer in a roasting tin or shallow ovenproof dish in which they fit snugly. Tuck the bay leaves around them.

2 Mix together the wine and honey and pour over the plums. Roast in a preheated oven, 220°C (425°F), Gas Mark 7, for 10–15 minutes or until the plums begin to colour but still retain their shape.

3 Grate the ginger and put it in a small heavy-based saucepan, scraping the gratings from the board and grater into the pan. Add the sugar and water. Heat gently, stirring until the sugar dissolves, then bring to the boil and boil for 1 minute. Strain into a clean pan.

4 Add the chopped chocolate to the pan and leave until melted, stirring frequently until smooth. If the chocolate doesn't melt, heat it through gently. Stir in the crème fraîche.

5 To serve, warm the sauce through gently. Transfer the plums to serving dishes, spoon over the cooking juices and serve with the sauce.

Upside-down chocolate and peach pots

Baked in individual dishes, this recipe makes a slightly more elegant variation on a classic 'upside-down' pudding.

PREPARATION TIME: 20 minutes

COOKING TIME: 20 minutes

OVEN TEMPERATURE: 190°C (375°F), Gas Mark 5

SERVES 6

125 g (4 oz) unsalted butter, plus extra for greasing

2 small ripe peaches or nectarines

200 g (7 oz) plain chocolate, broken up

2 eggs

40 g (1½ oz) light muscovado sugar

100 g (3½ oz) ratafia biscuits, crushed

50 g (2 oz) self-raising flour

4 tablespoons Amaretto liqueur

1 quantity Glossy Chocolate Syrup, to serve (see page 10)

1 Lightly butter 6 150 ml (¼ pint) ramekin or shallow ovenproof dishes and line the bases with circles of greaseproof paper. Halve and stone the fruit and cut one into 12 thin slices. Place 2 slices, side by side, in the base of each dish. Finely chop the remaining fruit. Melt the chocolate with the butter.

2 Beat together the eggs and sugar until smooth, then stir in the melted chocolate mixture, crushed biscuits, flour and chopped fruit, stirring gently until everything is evenly combined.

3 Spoon the mixture over the fruit slices in the dishes. Level the surfaces and place in a roasting tin. Bake in a preheated oven, 190°C (375°F), Gas Mark 5, for about 20 minutes until just firm to the touch. Leave to stand for 5 minutes. Stir the liqueur into the chocolate syrup in a small pan and heat through gently.

4 Loosen the edges of the dishes with a sharp knife and invert the puddings on to serving plates. Drizzle the syrup over and around the puddings and serve warm.

Baby chocolate puddings with nougat sauce

The filling in these little puddings melts into a fabulous sauce, which oozes out irresistibly when you cut through the dark chocolate case.

PREPARATION TIME: 25 minutes

COOKING TIME: 30 minutes

OVEN TEMPERATURE: 180°C (350°F), Gas Mark 4

SERVES 6

125 g (4 oz) unsalted butter, plus extra for greasing

100 g (3½ oz) plain chocolate, broken up

100 g (3½ oz) light muscovado sugar

2 eggs

250 g (8 oz) self-raising flour

25 g (1 oz) cocoa powder

100 g (3½ oz) nougat, chopped into small pieces

25 g (1 oz) raisins

100 g (3½ oz) white chocolate, chopped

pouring cream, to serve

1 Lightly butter 6 150 ml (¼ pint) metal pudding moulds. Melt the plain chocolate in a large bowl with 100 g (3½ oz) of the butter. Leave to cool slightly.

2 Stir in the sugar and eggs. Sift the flour and cocoa powder over the mixture and stir together to make a soft paste. Spoon two-thirds of the mixture into the prepared tins and spread up the sides with the back of a teaspoon.

3 Cut the remaining butter into small pieces and mix with the nougat, raisins and white chocolate. Spoon the mixture evenly into the centres of the puddings.

4 Cover each pudding with the remaining dark chocolate mixture so that the filling is completely enclosed.

5 Place the moulds in a roasting tin and pour in boiling water to a depth of 2 cm (¾ inch). Cover the tin with foil, securing the ends under the rim. Bake in a preheated oven, 180°C (350°F), Gas Mark 4, for 25–30 minutes until the puddings are just firm to the touch. Leave them to stand for 5 minutes, then loosen the edges with a knife and invert them on to serving plates. Serve with pouring cream.

Sunken torte with orange liqueur cream

This chocolate cake rises during baking only to sink again as it cools. Don't be put off: the moist density of the mixture makes it utterly delicious.

PREPARATION TIME: 20 minutes

COOKING TIME: 30 minutes

OVEN TEMPERATURE: 160°C (325°F), Gas Mark 3

SERVES 8

250 g (8 oz) plain chocolate, broken up

125 g (4 oz) unsalted butter

1 teaspoon vanilla extract

6 medium eggs, separated

125 g (4 oz) light muscovado sugar

250 ml (8 fl oz) Greek yogurt

finely grated rind and juice of ½ orange

2 tablespoons orange liqueur

2 tablespoons icing sugar

chocolate curls, to decorate

1 Grease and line a 23 cm (9 inch) spring-form or loose-based cake tin with greaseproof paper, then grease the paper. Melt the chocolate with the butter in a small bowl and stir in the vanilla extract.

2 Whisk the egg yolks with 100 g (3½ oz) of the sugar in a large bowl for 3–4 minutes until the mixture leaves a trail when the whisk is lifted from the bowl. Fold in the chocolate mixture.

3 Whisk the egg whites in a clean bowl until peaking. Gradually whisk in the remaining sugar. Fold a quarter of the whisked whites into the chocolate mixture to lighten it, then fold in the remainder.

4 Turn into the tin and bake in a preheated oven, 160°C (325°F), Gas Mark 3, for 30 minutes or until well risen and springy.

5 Beat together the yogurt, orange rind and juice, liqueur and icing sugar until smooth, then chill. Cool the cake in the tin for 10 minutes before serving with the orange cream and chocolate curls.

Sunken torte with orange liqueur cream

Desserts *Chocolate desserts usually take a little longer to prepare than puddings, but they can be made well in advance, which is a distinct advantage if you're entertaining. Some of the recipes in this chapter give you the opportunity to show off your chocolate skills with piped or sculptured decorations or chocolate cases made using melted chocolate. Again, these can be done well in advance while you're in a relaxed frame of mind, taking the pressure off you at the last minute. If you do make cases or decorations, keep them in a very cool place, or in the refrigerator if the weather's warm. Protected in a plastic container, they'll keep well for up to a week.*

There are also several ice creams and frozen desserts on the following pages that are fabulous for entertaining. Buy an attractive freezerproof serving dish so that you can freeze and serve the dessert in it. For the best texture and flavour, transfer iced desserts to the refrigerator about thirty minutes before serving so that they have a chance to soften.

Chocolate and passion fruit roulade

Chocolate roulades have a soft, squidgy texture and a sugary crust, which cracks when it is rolled up so it looks craggy, moist and appealing.

PREPARATION TIME: 20 minutes, plus cooling

COOKING TIME: 20 minutes

OVEN TEMPERATURE: 180°C (350°F), Gas Mark 4

SERVES 8

175 g (6 oz) plain chocolate, broken up

5 eggs, separated

125 g (4 oz) caster sugar, plus extra to sprinkle

4 passion fruit, halved and scooped out

4 tablespoons orange curd

225 ml (8 fl oz) double cream

chocolate curls, to decorate

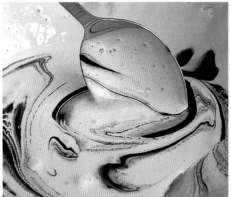

1 Grease and line a 33 x 23 cm (13 x 9 inch) Swiss roll tin with greaseproof paper, then grease the paper. Melt the chocolate in a small bowl.

2 Using an electric whisk, beat together the yolks and sugar for about 3–4 minutes until thickened and pale. Using a metal spoon, fold in the melted chocolate.

3 Whisk the egg whites in a clean bowl until peaking but not stiff. Fold about a quarter of the whisked whites into the chocolate mixture to lighten it, then fold in the remainder. Spread the mixture gently into the corners of the tin.

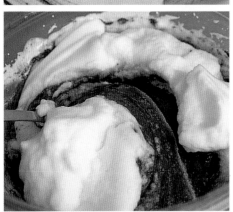

4 Bake in a preheated oven, 180°C (350°F), Gas Mark 4, for about 20 minutes until risen and just firm. Invert the roulade on to a sheet of greaseproof paper sprinkled with caster sugar and peel away the lining paper. Cover and leave to cool.

5 Add the passion fruit pulp to the orange curd and mix. Lightly whip the cream.

6 Spread the cream just to the edges of the roulade. Spoon the passion fruit mixture over the top, then roll up the roulade, using the paper. Turn on to a plate, join underneath, and scatter the curls over it.

Chocolate and passion fruit roulade

Poached pear and vanilla tart
A delicious blend of crisp biscuity pastry, smooth sweet ganache and fresh tangy pears. Keep an eye on the pears while they're poaching as cooking times will vary.

PREPARATION TIME: 40 minutes, plus cooling

COOKING TIME: 35 minutes

OVEN TEMPERATURE: 200°C (400°F), Gas Mark 6

SERVES 10

1 quantity Crisp Chocolate Pastry
(see page 17)

1.2 kg (2½ lb) firm ripe pears (e.g. Conference)

1 tablespoon lemon juice

50 g (2 oz) caster sugar

1 teaspoon vanilla bean paste or 2 teaspoons
vanilla extract

½ quantity White Chocolate Ganache
(see page 16)

½ teaspoon cornflour

1 tablespoon vodka

1 Thinly roll out the pastry on a lightly floured surface and use it to line a 25 cm (10 inch) loose-based flan tin, 2.5 cm (1 inch) deep (see page 17). Line the pastry case with greaseproof paper and fill with baking beans, then bake blind in a preheated oven, 200°C (400°F), Gas Mark 6, for 15 minutes. Remove the paper and beans and bake for a further 5 minutes. Leave to cool.

2 Peel, quarter and core the pears and put them in a large bowl of water with the lemon juice. Dissolve the sugar in 100 ml (3½ fl oz) water in a large frying pan. Add the vanilla and a third of the pear quarters and cover with a lid. Poach gently for 6–8 minutes until tender. Remove with a slotted spoon, drain and reserve. Add the remaining pears to the pan, cook for a further 6–8 minutes and remove with a slotted spoon to a food processor, reserving the juices. Blend the pears to a smooth paste.

3 Spoon the chocolate ganache into the pastry case and spread with the pear purée. Thinly slice the remaining pears and arrange them in overlapping slices over the purée.

4 Blend the cornflour with a little of the poaching juices in a small pan. Blend in the remaining juices and cook gently for about 2 minutes until thickened. Stir in the vodka and use the mixture to glaze the tart. Chill until ready to serve.

White chocolate and cherry tart
A luxurious blend of creamy white chocolate and tangy cherries. If you're making it a day in advance, halve the quantity of gelatine, as it will firm up overnight.

PREPARATION TIME: 35 minutes

COOKING TIME: 20 minutes

OVEN TEMPERATURE: 180°C (350°F), Gas Mark 4

SERVES 10

1 quantity Crisp Chocolate Pastry
  (see page 17)

425 g (14 oz) can pitted black cherries in syrup

1 teaspoon powdered gelatine

100 ml (3½ fl oz) milk

250 g (8 oz) white chocolate, broken up

250 g (8 oz) Greek yogurt

1 egg white

25 g (1 oz) caster sugar

½ teaspoon cornflour

1 Thinly roll out the pastry on a lightly floured surface and use it to line a 23 cm (9 inch) loose-based flan tin, 2.5 cm (1 inch) deep (see page 17). Line with greaseproof paper and fill with baking beans, then bake blind in a preheated oven, 180°C (350°F), Gas Mark 4, for 15 minutes. Remove the beans and paper and bake for a further 5 minutes. Leave to cool.

2 Drain the cherries, reserving the syrup. Sprinkle the gelatine over the milk in a small heatproof bowl and leave to soak for 5 minutes. Melt the chocolate in a large bowl.

3 Stand the gelatine bowl in a saucepan containing 1 cm (½ inch) of simmering water. Leave for about 2 minutes until the gelatine has dissolved, then stir it into the melted chocolate. Stir in the yogurt and leave for about 30 minutes until the mixture begins to thicken.

4 Whisk the egg white in a clean bowl until stiff, then gradually whisk in the sugar. Fold into the chocolate mixture and turn it into the pastry case. Scatter the cherries over the top.

5 Mix the cornflour in a small pan with 1 tablespoon of the cherry syrup. Add a further 5 tablespoons syrup and cook for about 1 minute until thickened. Drizzle the syrup over the tart.

Peppered panna cotta with strawberry sauce

The idea of flavouring fruit dishes with pepper is a traditional one, so don't be put off. It can be omitted, though, for a milder flavour.

PREPARATION TIME: 20 minutes, plus setting

COOKING TIME: 3 minutes

SERVES 6

1 teaspoon pink peppercorns in brine
1 teaspoon powdered gelatine
250 g (8 oz) mascarpone cheese
300 ml (½ pint) double cream
150 g (5 oz) white chocolate, chopped
300 g (10 oz) strawberries
2–3 tablespoons icing sugar

To decorate
piped chocolate scribbles (see page 7)
fresh strawberries

1 Rinse and dry the peppercorns. Use a pestle and mortar to crush them until fairly finely ground. Sprinkle the gelatine over 2 tablespoons water in a small bowl and leave it to stand for 5 minutes. Lightly oil 6 125 ml (4 fl oz) dariole moulds.

2 Put the mascarpone in a medium-sized saucepan with the cream and crushed peppercorns and bring just to the boil, stirring until smooth. Remove from the heat and add the gelatine. Stir until dissolved (about 1 minute) then tip in the chocolate. Leave until melted.

3 Pour into a jug and then pour it into the moulds, stirring between each pour to distribute the peppercorns evenly. Chill for several hours or overnight until set.

4 Blend the strawberries in a food processor with a little icing sugar and 1 tablespoon water until smooth. Test for sweetness, adding more sugar if necessary.

5 Loosen the edges of the moulds with a knife and shake them out on to plates. Spoon the sauce around and decorate with piped chocolate scribbles and strawberries.

Peppered panna cotta with strawberry sauce

Chocolate posset
Rich, creamy and mildly flavoured with a fresh herb syrup, these little chocolate pots are delicious with buttery shortbread biscuits.

PREPARATION TIME: 10 minutes, plus standing

COOKING TIME: 3 minutes

SERVES 6

50 g (2 oz) caster sugar

4 bay leaves

10 long thyme sprigs

150 ml (¼ pint) water

150 g (5 oz) plain chocolate, chopped

300 ml (½ pint) double cream

cocoa powder or icing sugar, for dusting

1 Put the sugar, bay leaves and thyme sprigs in a medium-sized heavy-based saucepan with the water and heat gently until the sugar dissolves. Bring to the boil, remove from the heat and leave to infuse for 20 minutes. Lift out the herbs and reheat the syrup until it is hot but not boiling.

2 Remove the saucepan from the heat and tip in the chocolate. Leave for 3–4 minutes, stirring frequently until the chocolate has melted.

3 Add the cream and stir until smooth. Pour the mixture into 6 tiny cups or dishes and chill for 4 hours or until lightly set. Dust with cocoa powder or icing sugar and serve with dessert biscuits.

Variation

Use white chocolate instead of plain and reduce the sugar to 25 g (1 oz). Add 2 teaspoons lemon juice to the syrup.

White chocolate and blueberry trifle

Trifle has a way of reinventing itself, and this version is one of the best. Gin goes perfectly with the fruit and the lemony cream.

PREPARATION TIME: 20 minutes, plus chilling

COOKING TIME: 2 minutes

SERVES 6–8

600 ml (1 pint) milk

4 egg yolks

3 tablespoons cornflour

300 g (10 oz) white chocolate, chopped

300 g (10 oz) blueberries

4 tablespoons gin or vodka

4 tablespoons icing sugar, plus extra for dusting

300 g (10 oz) bought or homemade Madeira cake

300 ml (½ pint) double cream

2 tablespoons lemon juice

plain or white chocolate caraque, to decorate (see page 6)

1 Bring the milk almost to the boil in a medium-sized heavy-based saucepan. Beat together the egg yolks and cornflour in a bowl. Pour the milk over the yolks, stirring, then return the saucepan to the heat. Cook briefly until the mixture is thickened and bubbling. Stir in the chocolate until melted, and leave to cool.

2 Reserve 50 g (2 oz) of the blueberries. Pierce the remainder with a fork and add the liqueur and 2 tablespoons of the icing sugar. Stir then leave for 5 minutes.

3 Cut the cake into chunks and scatter them in a large glass dish or individual dishes. Sprinkle with the soaked berries, then pile the cooled custard on top.

4 Whip the cream with the remaining icing sugar and the lemon juice until softly peaking. Spoon over the custard. Scatter with the reserved blueberries and chocolate caraque. Serve dusted with icing sugar.

Chocolate Amaretto jellies

Try these delicious 'grown-up' jellies, laced with almond liqueur. They're set in little jelly moulds, but you could use small metal pudding moulds instead.

PREPARATION TIME: 15 minutes, plus setting

COOKING TIME: 5 minutes

SERVES 8

1 tablespoon powdered gelatine

300 g (10 oz) plain chocolate, broken up

150 ml (¼ pint) Amaretto liqueur

450 ml (¾ pint) milk

100 ml (3½ fl oz) double cream

1 quantity Glossy Chocolate Syrup
(see page 10)

1 Sprinkle the gelatine over 3 tablespoons water in a small bowl and leave to soak for 5 minutes. Melt the chocolate in a large bowl with the liqueur, stirring frequently until smooth.

2 Bring the milk just to the boil and remove from the heat. Pour the warm milk over the chocolate, whisking well until completely smooth.

3 Add the soaked gelatine and stir for 1 minute until dissolved. Divide among 8 125–150 ml (4–5 fl oz) individual moulds and leave to cool. Chill for at least 6 hours, preferably overnight, until just firm.

4 To serve, half-fill a small bowl with very hot water and dip a mould up to the rim in the water for 2 seconds. Invert on to a serving plate and, gripping both plate and mould, shake the jelly out on the plate. Lift away the mould and repeat with the other jellies.

5 Pour a little cream around each jelly, then drizzle a tablespoonful of syrup through it. Lightly swirl the syrup into the cream to decorate.

Chocolate Amaretto jellies

White chocolate and Earl Grey parfait

Unlike ice cream, frozen parfaits don't need churning during freezing, which makes them a great alternative if you haven't got an electric ice cream maker.

PREPARATION TIME: 25 minutes, plus freezing

COOKING TIME: 10 minutes

SERVES 8

6 Earl Grey teabags

200 g (7 oz) white chocolate, chopped

50 g (2 oz) caster sugar

4 egg yolks

300 ml (½ pint) double cream

2 tablespoons lemon juice

plain or white chocolate caraque, to decorate (see page 6)

1 Pour 150 ml (¼ pint) boiling water into a small jug. Drop in the teabags and infuse for 3 minutes. Squeeze out the bags and immediately add the chocolate to the liquid. Leave for 2 minutes, then stir lightly to make a smooth sauce. Bring a medium-sized saucepan of water to the boil, then reduce the heat to a simmer.

2 Gently heat the sugar in a small heavy-based pan with 4 tablespoons water until the sugar dissolves. Bring to the boil and boil rapidly, without stirring, until the syrup registers 115°C (239°F) on a sugar thermometer. Alternatively, drop a teaspoonful of the syrup into a bowl of cold water and leave for 10 seconds. If the syrup can be moulded into a soft ball, it's ready. Remove from the heat.

3 Use an electric whisk to beat the egg yolks in a large bowl until frothy. Place over the simmering water, making sure the base of the bowl doesn't touch the water. Slowly whisk in the sugar syrup.

4 In a separate bowl, whisk together the cream and tea mixture until softly peaking. Fold the cream into the egg mixture and pour it into 8 small freezerproof serving dishes. Freeze for at least 3 hours or until firm. Transfer to the refrigerator 30 minutes before serving, and decorate with chocolate caraque.

Eton mess
Making the meringues yourself gives by far the best results in this fabulous dessert. You can use good quality bought ones if you prefer, but avoid the cheap, powdery ones.

PREPARATION TIME: 20 minutes

COOKING TIME: 1 hour

OVEN TEMPERATURE: 140°C (275°F), Gas Mark 1

SERVES 6

2 egg whites

100 g (3½ oz) caster sugar

½ quantity White Chocolate Ganache
   (see page 16)

200 g (7 oz) Greek yogurt

350 g (11½ oz) fresh raspberries

1 Line a large baking sheet with nonstick baking paper. Whisk the egg whites in a clean bowl until stiff. Gradually whisk in the sugar, a tablespoonful at a time, whisking well after each addition, until the meringue is stiff and glossy. Put spoonfuls on the baking sheet and bake in a preheated oven, 140°C (275°F), Gas Mark 1, for about 1 hour until crisp. Transfer to a wire rack to cool.

2 Mix together the ganache and yogurt. Take 75 g (3 oz) of the meringues (putting the rest in an air-tight container to keep) and crumble them into a large bowl. If they're a bit sticky in the centre, just pull them apart. Stir in the raspberries.

3 Add the ganache mixture and lightly fold the ingredients together. Spoon into 6 glasses and chill until ready to serve.

Coconut creams with chocolate berries

Make these creamy custards a day in advance so they have plenty of time to chill and firm up, but leave the chocolate berries until the day you need them.

PREPARATION TIME: 15 minutes, plus chilling

COOKING TIME: 50 minutes

OVEN TEMPERATURE: 150°C (300°F), Gas Mark 2

SERVES 6

6 egg yolks

50 g (2 oz) caster sugar

1 teaspoon cornflour

400 ml (14 fl oz) can coconut milk

300 ml (½ pint) single cream

50 g (2 oz) plain chocolate, broken up

100 ml (3½ fl oz) crème de cassis

250 g (8 oz) blackberries

1 Lightly oil 6 150 ml (¼ pint) metal pudding moulds or ramekin dishes. (If you use ramekin dishes, line the bases with circles of greaseproof paper.) Put the egg yolks, sugar and cornflour in a large bowl and whisk together lightly. Bring the coconut milk and cream to the boil in a saucepan and pour over the yolks mixture, whisking well.

2 Divide the mixture between the moulds and place them in a roasting tin. Pour in boiling water to a depth of 2 cm (¾ inch). Cover the tin with foil and bake in a preheatead oven, 150°C (300°F), Gas Mark 2, for about 50 minutes or until the custards feel very softly set. Remove from the roasting tin and leave to cool. Chill until ready to serve.

3 To make the sauce, melt the chocolate in a small bowl with the liqueur and leave to cool slightly. Stir in the blackberries.

4 Loosen the edges of the moulds with a sharp knife and invert them on to serving plates. Serve with the chocolate berries spooned around.

Barely set cheesecake
Unlike many baked cheesecakes, this one's soft and creamy and smooth on the palate. Don't overcook it or the texture will become too firm.

PREPARATION TIME: 20 minutes

COOKING TIME: 25 minutes

OVEN TEMPERATURE: 160°C (325°F), Gas Mark 3

SERVES 8

50 g (2 oz) unsalted butter

200 g (7 oz) digestive biscuits, crushed

200 g (7 oz) plain chocolate, broken up

200 g (7 oz) white chocolate, broken up

400 g (13 oz) full-fat soft cheese

3 eggs

150 ml (¼ pint) double cream

icing sugar, for dusting

chocolate-dipped cherries, to decorate (see page 7)

1 Melt the butter in a medium-sized saucepan and add the biscuit crumbs, stirring until they are evenly coated. Pack the mixture into the base of an 18 cm (7 inch) spring-form or loose-based cake tin.

2 Melt the plain and white chocolate in separate bowls. Beat the soft cheese in a bowl until smooth. Gradually beat in the eggs and then the cream. Spoon half the mixture into a separate bowl.

3 Stir the plain chocolate into one of the cheese mixtures, mixing in 2 tablespoons water until smooth. Turn the mixture into the tin. Stir the white chocolate into the other cheese mixture with 2 tablespoons water. Spoon over the plain chocolate mixture and level the surface.

4 Bake in a preheated oven, 160°C (325°F), Gas Mark 3, for 25 minutes until the cheesecake has set around the edges but is still very wobbly in the centre. Leave to cool in the tin.

5 Loosen the edges of the cheesecake with a knife and transfer it to a serving plate. Dust with icing sugar and decorate with chocolate-dipped cherries.

Chocolate mousse with mulled apricots

Set these chocolate mousses in little dishes if you haven't the time to make the cases, and spoon the fruits around them.

PREPARATION TIME: 35 minutes, plus setting

COOKING TIME: 5 minutes

SERVES 6

50 g (2 oz) golden caster sugar

2 cinnamon sticks

1 teaspoon whole cloves

150 ml (¼ pint) dry white wine

500 g (1 lb) fresh apricots, halved

2 tablespoons brandy

300 g (10 oz) plain chocolate, broken up

1 tablespoon golden syrup

4 egg whites

1 Heat the sugar, cinnamon, cloves and wine until the sugar dissolves. Add the apricots and cover. Poach gently for 5 minutes until the apricots are tender but still retain their shape. Stir in the brandy, and cool.

2 Cut out 6 20 x 7 cm (8 x 2¾ inch) rectangles of acetate. Slightly overlap the ends and secure with tape. Put on a baking sheet lined with greaseproof paper. Melt 100 g (3½ oz) of the chocolate. Spoon a little into the base of each acetate shape.

3 Holding an acetate shape steady, brush the chocolate up the sides to make a case. Add more chocolate if necessary to make sure the acetate is covered. Make the other cases in the same way. Chill until set.

4 Melt the remaining chocolate with the syrup and 1 tablespoon of water. Whisk the egg whites in a clean bowl until just peaking. Stir a quarter of the whisked whites into the mixture to lighten it, then gently fold in the remainder.

5 Cut through the adhesive tape with a sharp knife, then carefully remove the acetate. Spoon the mousse into the cases and chill. Serve with the mulled apricots.

Chilli chocolate marquise with poached fruits

This quick and easy dessert is laced with punchy ingredients, including red chilli and tequila, giving it quite a kick.

PREPARATION TIME: 20 minutes, plus chilling

COOKING TIME: 5 minutes

SERVES 6–8

325 g (11 oz) plain chocolate, broken up

75 g (3 oz) unsalted butter, softened

1 hot red chilli, deseeded and finely chopped

100 g (3½ oz) icing sugar

2 egg whites

200 ml (7 fl oz) crème fraîche

1 small mango, halved and stoned

300 g (10 oz) lychees, peeled and stoned

15 g (½ oz) golden caster sugar

6 tablespoons tequila or rum

100 g (3½ oz) blueberries

1 Line a 500 g (1 lb) loaf tin with clingfilm, fitting it carefully into the corners. Melt the chocolate in a medium-sized bowl and leave to cool.

2 In a separate bowl, beat together the butter, chilli and 50 g (2 oz) of the icing sugar until smooth. Whisk the egg whites in a clean bowl until peaking and whisk in the remaining sugar. Stir the chocolate into the chilli butter and then the crème fraîche. Immediately fold in a quarter of the whisked whites to lighten the mixture, then fold in the remainder. Turn the mixture into the tin, level the surface and chill for at least 4 hours until firm.

3 Slice the mango and halve the lychees. Heat the sugar in a small saucepan with 100 ml (3½ fl oz) water until the sugar dissolves. Bring to the boil and boil for 3–5 minutes until the liquid turns syrupy.

4 Remove the syrup from the heat and stir in all the fruits. Leave to cool, then turn the fruit into a bowl and stir in the liqueur.

5 Invert the marquise on to a plate and peel away the clingfilm. Cut into thick slices, transfer to serving plates and top with the poached fruits.

Creamy chocolate caramels

These chocolate caramels retain the irresistibly silky, wobbly texture of classic crème caramels but benefit from the addition of smooth, dark chocolate.

PREPARATION TIME: 15 minutes

COOKING TIME: 30 minutes

OVEN TEMPERATURE: 160°C (325°F), Gas Mark 3

SERVES 8

300 g (10 oz) granulated sugar

600 ml (1 pint) milk

150 g (5 oz) plain chocolate, chopped

4 eggs

4 egg yolks

1 Put 250 g (8 oz) of the sugar in a heavy-based saucepan with 4 tablespoons water and heat gently, stirring until the sugar dissolves. Bring to the boil and boil without stirring for about 10 minutes until the syrup starts to caramelize. Gently swirl the pan to ensure the syrup browns evenly.

2 Continue to cook the syrup until it is deep golden, but watch closely as it will brown quickly. Immerse the base of the pan in cold water to prevent further cooking. Working quickly, pour the syrup into 8 150 ml (¼ pint) ramekin dishes, tilting each so the syrup comes up the sides.

3 Put the milk in a heavy-based saucepan with the chopped chocolate and heat gently until the chocolate has melted. Whisk together the eggs and yolks with the remaining sugar and add the chocolate milk. Strain into a large jug and pour into the ramekins. Place them in a roasting tin and pour hot water into the tin to a depth of 1 cm (½ inch).

4 Bake in a preheated oven, 160°C (325°F), Gas Mark 3, for 20 minutes or until just set. The custards should wobble when the tin is gently shaken. Cool, then chill until ready to serve. Run the tip of a sharp knife around the edge of each dish and invert on to serving plates.

Variation

For white chocolate caramels, omit the sugar in the custard and use white chocolate instead of the plain.

Drizzled sorbet in chocolate cases *Sculptured*

chocolate cases make perfect containers for scoops of chocolate sorbet. Pile the sorbet into the cases and drizzle with the liqueur and cream.

PREPARATION TIME: 25 minutes, plus freezing

COOKING TIME: 10 minutes

SERVES 6

250 g (8 oz) light muscovado sugar

150 g (5 oz) cocoa powder

250 g (8 oz) plain chocolate, broken up

6 tablespoons coffee liqueur

6 tablespoons double cream

1 Put 1 litre (1¾ pints) cold water in a heavy-based saucepan with the sugar and cocoa powder and cook slowly, stirring until smooth. Reduce the heat to low and cook gently, stirring frequently until thick and glossy and thickly coating the back of the wooden spoon, rather like a custard. Leave to cool.

2 Turn the mixture into a plastic tub and freeze for about 4 hours until mushy. Blend until smooth, then return to the freezer for a further 2 hours until frozen.

3 To make the cases, cut out 6 15 cm (5 inch) squares of nonstick baking paper. Press into 6 sections of a 12-section muffin tray, securing to the base with pieces of masking tape and spacing them apart so they're not bunched up.

4 Melt the chocolate and put a generous dessertspoonful into the base of each paper lining, spreading it up the sides with a small spoon and bringing it up to the points of the squares. Make sure the paper is thickly covered with chocolate. Chill for about 30 minutes until brittle.

5 Carefully peel away the paper and return the cases to the refrigerator. To serve, put small scoops of sorbet in the cases and pour a tablespoon of liqueur and cream over each.

Light and dark chocolate truffle

A quick and easy but impressive-looking dessert for entertaining. Allow plenty of time to steep the apricots in the liqueur so that they plump up.

PREPARATION TIME: 30 minutes, plus soaking

SERVES 10

200 g (7 oz) no-soak apricots, roughly chopped

6 tablespoons Drambuie or brandy

200 g (7 oz) plain chocolate, broken up

300 g (10 oz) white chocolate, broken up

450 ml (¾ pint) double cream

jagged chocolate brittle, to decorate
(see page 7)

cocoa powder, for dusting

1 Put the apricots and liqueur in a small saucepan and heat gently until the liqueur starts to bubble around the edges of the pan. Turn the fruit and liquid into a small bowl, cover and leave to soak for at least 4 hours.

2 Line a 1 kg (2 lb) loaf tin with clingfilm, making sure it fits into the corners. Let the excess overhang the sides of the tin.

3 Melt the plain and white chocolate in separate, medium-sized bowls. Divide the cream between 2 bowls and whisk each until slightly thickened but not holding its shape. Stir one lot of cream into the white chocolate and the other into the plain, adding 4–5 tablespoons hot water to the plain so the mixtures are about the same consistency.

4 Stir the apricots into the white chocolate cream, draining off any unabsorbed liqueur into the plain. Spread half the plain chocolate cream into the tin and spoon over half the white chocolate cream. Spoon over the remaining plain chocolate cream. Finally, add the remaining white chocolate cream.

5 Chill for at least 4 hours or overnight until firm. To serve, invert on to a long, flat plate and decorate with the jagged chocolate brittle and a dusting of cocoa powder.

Turkish delight and chocolate ripple *Swirling*

Turkish delight and chocolate sauces into softly set ice cream makes a fabulous concoction for scooping into glasses or ice cream cones.

PREPARATION TIME: 30 minutes, plus freezing

COOKING TIME: 10 minutes

SERVES 6–8

300 ml (½ pint) milk

4 egg yolks

100 g (3½ oz) caster sugar

1 teaspoon cornflour

300 ml (½ pint) double cream

200 g (7 oz) rose-flavoured Turkish delight

100 g (3½ oz) plain chocolate, broken up

25 g (1 oz) unsalted butter

1 Heat the milk in a medium-sized heavy-based saucepan until almost boiling. Beat together the egg yolks, 75 g (3 oz) of the sugar and the cornflour in a bowl. Add the hot milk, stirring. Return the mixture to the pan and cook over a very gentle heat, stirring with a wooden spoon until slightly thickened. Turn the mixture into a bowl, cover with a circle of greaseproof paper and leave to cool.

2 Whip the cream until it just holds its shape. Stir it into the custard and turn the mixture into a shallow freezer container. Freeze for 4–6 hours until softly set.

3 Alternatively, if you have an ice cream maker, stir the cream into the custard and churn until softly set. Transfer to a shallow freezer container.

4 Meanwhile, make the sauces. Cut up the Turkish delight with scissors and blend in a food processor with 100 ml (3½ fl oz) cold water. Transfer to a small pan and cook gently until smooth and syrupy.

5 Put the chocolate in a small pan and add the butter, the remaining sugar and 2 tablespoons water. Heat gently to make a smooth sauce.

6 When the sauces are cool but still runny, spoon them over the ice cream and fold in until rippled. Re-freeze until firm.

Flaked lime and coconut ice cream
A fabulous 'make ahead' special dessert of sweet, tangy ice cream, interleaved with flaky bites of dark chocolate.

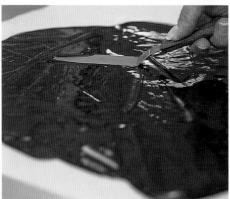

PREPARATION TIME: 30 minutes, plus freezing

COOKING TIME: 3 minutes

SERVES 8

6 egg yolks

175 g (6 oz) caster sugar

2 teaspoons cornflour

2 400 ml (14 fl oz) cans coconut milk

finely grated rind and juice of 4 limes

200 g (7 oz) plain chocolate, broken up

450 ml (¾ pint) double or whipping cream

cocoa powder, for dusting

1 Whisk together the egg yolks, sugar and cornflour. Bring the coconut milk almost to the boil in a pan and pour over the mixture, whisking well. Return to the pan and cook very gently, stirring until slightly thickened. Transfer to a bowl, cover with greaseproof paper and leave to cool. Stir in the lime rind and juice.

2 Melt the chocolate. Cut 2 lengths of nonstick baking paper, each 46 x 33 cm (18 x 13 inches). Spoon half the chocolate on to each sheet, spreading it as thinly as possible. Leave until beginning to set, then chill, bending the sheets if necessary.

3 Whip the cream until it just holds its shape. Stir into the custard and freeze for 4–6 hours until softly set.

4 Alternatively, if you have an ice cream maker, stir the cream into the custard and churn until softly set.

5 Peel the chocolate from the paper, breaking it into flakes. Reserve a handful. Spoon a quarter of the ice cream into a freezerproof dish and scatter with a third of the chocolate. Repeat the layering and arrange the reserved flakes on top. Freeze until firm and serve dusted with cocoa powder.

Flaked lime and coconut ice cream

Cakes, bakes and cookies *This chapter contains some of the most chocolaty cakes imaginable, including one that's made without flour, so it's perfect for those on a wheat-free diet. One of the secrets of a good chocolate cake is to keep baking time to a minimum: over-baked cakes quickly loose the moist, gooey texture that makes them so memorable.*

Although leftovers are unlikely, all the cakes in this chapter (with the exception of the brownies, choux buns and White Chocolate Summer Berry Cake) freeze well for a couple of months. Small cakes that go stale quickly, such as the muffins and scones, are best frozen once cooled, so you can simply warm them through whenever you fancy some. Chocolate biscuits are another favourite chocolate bake, but they are best eaten very fresh as they gradually loose their crisp texture during storage. If necessary, any softened biscuits can be briefly returned to a hot oven to restore their former crispness.

White chocolate summer berry cake
This creamy cake is packed with white chocolate and berries. The sponge can be made a day in advance and assembled a few hours before serving.

PREPARATION TIME: 40 minutes, plus cooling

COOKING TIME: 30 minutes

OVEN TEMPERATURE: 180°C (350°F), Gas Mark 4

SERVES 12

5 eggs

150 g (5 oz) caster sugar

150 g (5 oz) plain flour

75 g (3 oz) white chocolate, grated

50 g (2 oz) unsalted butter, melted

200 g (7 oz) strawberries

200 g (7 oz) raspberries

300 ml (½ pint) double cream

4 tablespoons orange liqueur

1 quantity White Chocolate Ganache (see page 16)

1 Grease and line the bases of 2 20 cm (8 inch) sandwich tins. Grease the paper. Beat the eggs and sugar in a heatproof bowl over a pan of hot water until the whisk leaves a trail when lifted from the bowl. Remove from the heat and whisk for a further 2 minutes.

2 Sift the flour over the mixture, sprinkle with the chocolate and fold in. Drizzle the melted butter over the mixture and fold in. Divide between the tins and bake in a preheated oven, 180°C (350°F), Gas Mark 4, for 25–30 minutes or until just firm. Transfer to a wire rack to cool.

3 Reserve a handful of the fruits and lightly mash the remainder. Whip the cream until just peaking. Halve each cake and drizzle with the liqueur. Spread one layer with a third of the whipped cream and then a third of the fruits. Repeat the layering, finishing with a cake layer.

4 Spread a little ganache over the cake to seal in any crumbs, then swirl over the remainder. Scatter with the reserved fruits.

White chocolate summer berry cake

Deliciously dark chocolate cake *Ground nuts replace the flour in this chocolate-packed treat, so even people who are avoiding wheat can tuck in.*

PREPARATION TIME: 20 minutes

COOKING TIME: 30 minutes

OVEN TEMPERATURE: 180°C (350°F), Gas Mark 4

SERVES 12

200 g (7 oz) plain chocolate, broken up

75 ml (3 fl oz) milk

175 g (6 oz) unsalted butter, very soft, almost melting

175 g (6 oz) caster sugar

200 g (7 oz) ground almonds or hazelnuts

5 eggs, separated

200 g (7 oz) chocolate hazelnut spread

cocoa powder, for dusting

1 Grease and line the bases of 2 18 cm (7 inch) sandwich tins with greaseproof paper. Grease the paper. Melt the chocolate with the milk in a small bowl.

2 Put the butter and sugar in a large bowl and beat to a soft paste. Stir the melted chocolate mixture, ground nuts and egg yolks into the paste until evenly combined.

3 Whisk the egg whites in a clean bowl until peaking. Use a large metal spoon to fold a quarter of the whites into the chocolate mixture to lighten it, then fold in the remainder.

4 Divide the mixture between the tins and level the surface. Bake in a preheated oven, 180°C (350°F), Gas Mark 4, for 30 minutes until just firm. Leave in the tins for 5 minutes, then invert on to a cooling rack lined with greaseproof paper. Leave to cool completely.

5 Sandwich the cakes together with the chocolate spread and dust lightly with cocoa powder.

White chocolate and lavender Madeira *Light,*
buttery and subtly flavoured, this is a good teatime cake to make when
lavender is coming into bloom.

PREPARATION TIME: 15 minutes

COOKING TIME: 40 minutes

OVEN TEMPERATURE: 180°C (350°F), Gas Mark 4

SERVES 8

150 g (5 oz) white chocolate, broken up

8 lavender sprigs

25 g (1 oz) caster sugar

125 g (4 oz) unsalted butter, softened

2 eggs, beaten

125 g (4 oz) self-raising flour

25 g (1 oz) ground almonds

icing sugar, for dusting

1 Grease and line the base and long sides of a 500 g (1 lb) loaf tin with a strip of greaseproof paper. Grease the paper. Melt the chocolate in a small bowl.

2 Pull the lavender flowers from the stalks and beat them in a bowl with the sugar and butter until smooth and creamy. (Discard the stalks.) Gradually beat in the eggs, adding a little of the flour to prevent curdling.

3 Stir in the melted chocolate. Sift the remaining flour over the bowl and gently fold in with the ground almonds.

4 Turn the mixture into the tin and level the surface. Bake in a preheated oven, 180°C (350°F), Gas Mark 4, for 40 minutes until risen and firm to the touch. Transfer to a wire rack to cool and serve generously dusted with icing sugar.

Moist and gooey chocolate cake

The secret of success is to get the baking time just right. Too long in the oven, and the texture will gradually become firm and lose its delicious gooeyness.

PREPARATION TIME: 30 minutes

COOKING TIME: 1 hour

OVEN TEMPERATURE: 160°C (325°F), Gas Mark 3

SERVES 14–16

400 g (13 oz) plain chocolate

175 g (6 oz) unsalted butter, softened

250 g (8 oz) light muscovado sugar

4 eggs

100 g (3½ oz) self-raising flour

50 g (2 oz) cocoa powder

100 g (3½ oz) ground almonds

300 ml (½ pint) double cream

250 g (8 oz) mascarpone cheese

1 Grease and line the base and sides of a 20 cm (8 inch) round cake tin. Grease the paper. Melt 250 g (8 oz) of the chocolate with 75 ml (3 fl oz) water in a small bowl. Beat together the butter and sugar until pale and creamy. Gradually beat in the eggs, adding a little of the flour if necessary to prevent curdling. Stir in the chocolate.

2 Sift the remaining flour and cocoa over the bowl. Add the almonds and fold all three gently into the cake mixture.

3 Turn the mixture into the tin and level the surface. Bake in a preheated oven, 160°C (325°F), Gas Mark 3, for about 1 hour or until risen and just firm to the touch. The centre should still be slightly sticky if pierced with a skewer. Cool in the tin.

4 Use a large knife to cut the cake into 3 layers. Very lightly whip the cream and use it to sandwich the cake layers on a serving plate. Melt the remaining chocolate in a small bowl.

5 Beat the mascarpone with 1 tablespoon boiling water. Beat in the melted chocolate and spread over the cake.

Moist and gooey chocolate cake

Drambuie fruit cake

Adding chocolate to a chunky fruit cake might seem a little overindulgent, but the results are absolutely delicious, particularly if the fruit has been steeped in alcohol before baking.

PREPARATION TIME: 25 minutes, plus soaking

COOKING TIME: 1½ hours

OVEN TEMPERATURE: 150°C (300°F), Gas Mark 2

SERVES 16

300 g (10 oz) sultanas

8 tablespoons Drambuie

250 g (8 oz) unsalted butter, softened

200 g (7 oz) light muscovado sugar

75 g (3 oz) stem ginger, finely chopped

4 eggs

200 g (7 oz) plain flour

25 g (1 oz) cocoa powder

1 teaspoon baking powder

175 g (6 oz) unblanched hazelnuts, roughly chopped

125 g (4 oz) plain chocolate, chopped

125 g (4 oz) milk chocolate, chopped

1 Put the sultanas and Drambuie in a bowl. Cover and leave for at least 4 hours or overnight. Grease and line the base and sides of a 20 cm (8 inch) round cake tin. Grease the paper.

2 Cream together the butter, sugar and ginger. Gradually beat in the eggs, adding a little of the flour to prevent curdling. Sift the remaining flour into the bowl with the cocoa powder and baking powder.

3 Reserve 25 g (1 oz) of the nuts and 25 g (1 oz) of each type of chopped chocolate and stir in the remainder with the sultanas and any soaking juices. Stir well until combined. Turn into the tin and level the surface.

4 Scatter with the reserved chocolate and nuts. Bake in a preheated oven, 150°C (300°F), Gas Mark 2, for about 1½ hours or until firm and a skewer inserted into the centre comes out clean. Leave to cool in the tin.

Torte with five spice syrup

Unlike most rich chocolate cakes, this one's 'poached' in the oven so that it stays amazingly moist. Drizzle with the syrup once you've transferred it to serving plates.

PREPARATION TIME: 20 minutes

COOKING TIME: 1 hour

OVEN TEMPERATURE: 160°C (325°F), Gas Mark 3

SERVES 12

275 g (9 oz) dark muscovado sugar

325 g (11 oz) plain chocolate, chopped

225 g (7½ oz) unsalted butter, diced

6 eggs

2 teaspoons five spice powder

chocolate ribbons, to decorate (see page 7)

cocoa powder, for dusting

1 Grease and line the base and sides of a 23 cm (9 inch) round cake tin with greaseproof paper. (Don't use a loose-based tin.) Grease the paper. Dissolve 150 g (5 oz) of the sugar in 100 ml (3½ fl oz) water. Bring to the boil and boil for 2 minutes until slightly syrupy. Remove from the heat, add the chocolate and butter and leave until melted, stirring frequently. (If the mixture cools before the chocolate and butter have melted, heat it through very gently.)

2 Whisk together the eggs and a further 75 g (3 oz) of the sugar until thickened, pale and mousse-like. Use a large metal spoon to fold in the cooled chocolate mixture then pour it into the tin.

3 Stand the tin in a roasting tin and pour in very hot water to a depth of 3.5 cm (1½ inches). Bake in a preheated oven, 160°C (325°F), Gas Mark 3, for about 1 hour until the cake is risen and wobbly in the centre. Lift the cake tin from the roasting tin and leave to cool completely.

4 Put the remaining sugar in a small saucepan with 100 ml (3½ fl oz) water and heat gently until the sugar dissolves. Bring to the boil and boil rapidly for 3 minutes. Stir in the five spice powder and cook gently for a further 1 minute.

5 Remove the cake from the tin and decorate with chocolate ribbons. Dust with cocoa powder and serve in wedges with the syrup spooned over.

Chocolate chip scones with citrus butter *These chocolate-studded scones are incredibly easy to make. You needn't even wait for them to cool – they're delicious served warm, split and buttered.*

PREPARATION TIME: 20 minutes

COOKING TIME: 12 minutes

OVEN TEMPERATURE: 220°C (425°F), Gas Mark 7

MAKES 8

225 g (8 oz) self-raising flour

1 teaspoon baking powder

125 g (4 oz) unsalted butter

100 g (3½ oz) plain or milk chocolate, finely chopped

50 g (2 oz) icing sugar

about 150 ml (¼ pint) milk, plus extra for glazing

finely grated rind of ½ small orange, plus 2 teaspoons juice

1 Grease a baking sheet. Sift the flour and baking powder into a bowl. Add 40 g (1½ oz) of the butter, cut into small pieces, and rub in with the fingertips until the mixture resembles fine breadcrumbs. Stir in the chocolate, 25 g (1 oz) of the sugar and 125 ml (4 fl oz) of the milk and mix to a soft dough, adding the remaining milk if the dough feels dry.

2 Turn the dough on to a lightly floured surface and roll out to 2 cm (¾ inch) thick. Use a 6 cm (2½ inch) cutter to cut out rounds, re-rolling and cutting out the trimmings as necessary.

3 Transfer to the baking sheet and brush with milk to glaze. Bake in a preheated oven, 220°C (425°F), Gas Mark 7, for 12 minutes until well risen and pale golden. Transfer to a wire rack to cool.

4 Meanwhile, beat together the remaining butter and sugar with the orange rind and juice and turn into a small serving dish, ready for spreading over the warm scones.

Chocolate chip scones with citrus butter

White chocolate and carrot cupcakes
These little cakes are perfect for an afternoon treat. Dust them lightly with icing sugar if you don't want the richness of the ganache topping.

PREPARATION TIME: 20 minutes

COOKING TIME: 20 minutes

OVEN TEMPERATURE: 180°C (350°F), Gas Mark 4

MAKES 12

125 g (4 oz) unsalted butter, softened

100 g (3½ oz) light muscovado sugar

150 g (5 oz) self-raising flour

1 teaspoon baking powder

75 g (3 oz) ground almonds

2 eggs

150 g (5 oz) carrots, grated

50 g (2 oz) raisins

125 g (4 oz) white chocolate, chopped

1 quantity White Chocolate Ganache
(see page 16)

white chocolate shavings, to decorate
(see page 6)

1 Line a 12-section muffin tray with paper muffin cases. Beat together the butter, sugar, flour, baking powder, ground almonds and eggs with a hand-held electric whisk until light and creamy.

2 Stir in the carrots, raisins and chocolate and divide the mixture between the paper cases.

3 Bake in a preheated oven, 180°C (350°F), Gas Mark 4, for about 20 minutes until risen and firm.

4 Leave to cool in the tin, then spread with the chocolate ganache and decorate with white chocolate shavings.

Chunky chocolate and blueberry muffins *Use chopped plain, milk or white chocolate rather than chocolate chips to make these muffins totally chunky and chocolaty.*

PREPARATION TIME: 12 minutes

COOKING TIME: 15 minutes

OVEN TEMPERATURE: 200°C (400°F), Gas Mark 6

MAKES 12

50 g (2 oz) cocoa powder

200 g (7 oz) self-raising flour

2 teaspoons baking powder

100 g (3½ oz) light muscovado sugar

125 g (4 oz) plain, milk or white chocolate, chopped

125 g (4 oz) blueberries

1 egg

200 ml (7 fl oz) milk

100 g (3½ oz) unsalted butter, melted

1 Line a 12-section muffin tray with paper muffin cases. Sift the cocoa powder, flour and baking powder into a large bowl and stir in the sugar. Add the chopped chocolate and blueberries.

2 Beat the egg with the milk and melted butter, and add to the dry ingredients, stirring them gently together until only just combined. You should still see specks of dry flour in the mixture.

3 Divide the mixture among the paper cases and bake in a preheated oven, 200°C (400°F), Gas Mark 6, for about 15 minutes until risen and firm. Serve slightly warm.

Chocolate cheesecake brownies

Instead of the classic sugary crust, these brownies are swirled with a delicious, marbly cheesecake topping.

PREPARATION TIME: 20 minutes

COOKING TIME: 30 minutes

OVEN TEMPERATURE: 190°C (375°F), Gas Mark 5

MAKES about 16 rectangles

300 g (10 oz) plain chocolate, broken up
125 g (4 oz) lightly salted butter
150 g (5 oz) light muscovado sugar
75 g (3 oz) self-raising flour
75 g (3 oz) ground almonds
4 eggs
300 g (10 oz) mild soft goats' cheese
75 g (3 oz) caster sugar
1 teaspoon vanilla extract

1 Grease and line the base and sides of a shallow 28 x 20 cm (11 x 8 inch) baking tin. Grease the paper. Melt the chocolate with the butter in a medium-sized bowl.

2 Beat together the sugar, flour, ground almonds and 3 of the eggs in a mixing bowl to make a paste. Beat in the melted chocolate mixture.

3 In a separate bowl, beat the goats' cheese until softened. Beat in the sugar, remaining egg and vanilla extract until smooth. Turn the chocolate mixture into the prepared tin, then spoon the cheese mixture on top.

4 Use a round-bladed knife to swirl the 2 mixtures gently together, lifting some of the chocolate mixture into the cheese topping, until lightly marbled. (Don't overwork the mixture or the flavours will completely merge together.)

5 Bake in a preheated oven, 190°C (375°F), Gas Mark 5, for about 30 minutes or until very softly set in the centre. Leave to cool in the tin, then serve cut into small rectangles.

Chocolate, apple and hazelnut slice *Use well-flavoured apples, such as crisp and juicy Coxes, for this tray-bake. It's lovely served freshly baked and warm but will keep well for several days.*

PREPARATION TIME: 20 minutes

COOKING TIME: 45 minutes

OVEN TEMPERATURE: 180°C (350°F), Gas Mark 4

SERVES 10

150 g (5 oz) plain chocolate, broken up

175 g (6 oz) unsalted butter, softened

100 g (3½ oz) caster sugar

1 teaspoon vanilla extract

200 g (7 oz) self-raising flour

1 teaspoon baking powder

½ teaspoon ground cloves

3 eggs

4 dessert apples

4 tablespoons black treacle

50 g (2 oz) hazelnuts, roughly chopped

1 Grease and line a shallow 23 cm (9 inch) square baking tin with greaseproof paper. Grease the paper. Melt the chocolate in a small bowl.

2 Beat together the butter, sugar, vanilla extract, flour, baking powder, cloves and eggs in a mixing bowl. Quarter and core the apples. Chop half into small pieces and thinly slice the remainder. Stir the chopped apples into the creamed mixture with the melted chocolate and 3 tablespoons of the black treacle.

3 Turn into the prepared tin and level the surface. Scatter the apple slices and hazelnuts over the surface and bake in a preheated oven, 180°C (350°F), Gas Mark 4, for 40–45 minutes until just firm.

4 Drizzle with the remaining treacle and serve warm or cold, cut into fingers.

Variation

Use ripe and juicy pears instead of the apples, and cinnamon or mixed spice in place of the cloves.

Sticky choux buns
Some recipes are best left as true classics, so just concentrate here on getting the perfect balance of crisp pastry, lightly sweetened cream and sweet, sticky chocolate topping.

PREPARATION TIME: 40 minutes

COOKING TIME: 30 minutes

OVEN TEMPERATURE: 200°C (400°F), Gas Mark 6

MAKES 12

65 g (2½ oz) plain flour

65 g (2½ oz) unsalted butter, diced

2 eggs, beaten

300 ml (½ pint) double cream

1 tablespoon icing sugar

150 g (5 oz) plain chocolate, chopped

1 tablespoon golden syrup

1 Lightly grease a large baking sheet and sprinkle with water. Sift the flour on to a sheet of greaseproof paper. Melt 50 g (2 oz) of the butter in a medium-sized saucepan with 150 ml (¼ pint) water. Bring to the boil and remove from the heat.

2 Tip in the flour and beat until the mixture forms a ball that comes away from the sides of the pan. Leave to cool for 2 minutes, then gradually beat in the eggs until smooth and glossy.

3 Pipe or spoon 7.5 cm (3 inch) long fingers of paste on to the baking sheet, spacing them slightly apart. Bake in a preheated oven, 200°C (400°F), Gas Mark 6, for 25 minutes until well risen and golden. Make a slit down the side of each bun and return to the oven for 3 minutes to dry. Transfer to a wire rack to cool.

4 Whip the cream with the icing sugar until just peaking. Spoon or pipe into the cooled buns.

5 Put the chocolate in a small heavy-based saucepan with the remaining butter, syrup and 2 tablespoons water. Heat very gently until the chocolate has melted. Leave to cool before spreading over the buns.

Chocolate-swirled raisin bread

A deliciously rich and buttery bread to serve for an unhurried weekend breakfast. Make sure the chocolate butter is cool before you spread it over the dough.

PREPARATION TIME: 30 minutes, plus proving

COOKING TIME: 45 minutes

OVEN TEMPERATURE: 200°C (400°F), Gas Mark 6

SERVES 10

125 g (4 oz) lightly salted butter
1 egg
150 ml (¼ pint) milk
2 teaspoons easy-blend yeast
425 g (14 oz) strong white bread flour
1½ teaspoons ground mixed spice
75 g (3 oz) golden caster sugar
150 g (5 oz) plain or milk chocolate, broken up
75 g (3 oz) raisins
50 g (2 oz) unblanched hazelnuts, chopped
icing sugar, for dusting

1 Melt 100 g (3½ oz) of the butter and mix with the egg and milk. Mix the yeast, flour, spice, sugar and liquid to a dough in a bowl. Knead for 10 minutes, then put in an oiled bowl and cover with clingfilm. Leave for 1–2 hours until doubled in size.

2 Butter a 1 kg (2 lb) loaf tin. Melt the chocolate and remaining butter. Turn the dough on to a floured surface and knead in the raisins. Leave to stand, covered with a cloth, for 10 minutes. Roll out to a rectangle 33 cm (13 inches) long and as wide as the length of the tin.

3 Spread the chocolate to within 2 cm (¾ inch) of the edges. Scatter with the nuts.

4 Roll up the dough, starting from a short end, and drop it into the tin with the join on top. Cover loosely with oiled clingfilm and leave in a warm place for 45 minutes or until risen above the rim.

5 Bake in a preheated oven, 200°C (400°F), Gas Mark 6, for 45 minutes until deep golden. Turn out, dust with sugar and cool.

Marsala, raisin and chocolate teabread

Before you make this cake, allow plenty of time to steep the raisins in the Marsala, ideally overnight so that they really plump up.

PREPARATION TIME: 20 minutes, plus soaking

COOKING TIME: 1 hour

OVEN TEMPERATURE: 160°C (325°F), Gas Mark 3

SERVES 10

100 g (3½ oz) raisins

7 tablespoons Marsala

250 g (8 oz) plain chocolate, broken up

175 ml (6 fl oz) milk

250 g (8 oz) dark muscovado sugar

150 g (5 oz) unsalted butter, softened

3 eggs, beaten

250 g (8 oz) self-raising flour

1 Put the raisins and 5 tablespoons of the Marsala in a small saucepan and heat gently until the Marsala bubbles. Turn into a small container and leave to soak for at least 4 hours or overnight.

2 Grease and line the base and sides of a 1 kg (2 lb) loaf tin with greaseproof paper so that it comes about 2 cm (¾ inch) above the rim. Grease the paper. Heat 200 g (7 oz) of the chocolate and the milk in a small pan until the chocolate melts. Leave to cool slightly.

3 Use an electric whisk to beat together the sugar and butter until light and fluffy. Gradually beat in the eggs, adding a little of the flour to prevent curdling. Sift the remaining flour into the bowl and fold in.

4 Stir in the chocolate mixture and steeped raisins, reserving any unabsorbed Marsala. Turn the mixture into the tin and bake in a preheated oven, 160°C (325°F), Gas Mark 3, for 50–60 minutes until just firm and a skewer inserted into the centre comes out clean. Transfer to a wire rack to cool.

5 Melt the remaining chocolate in a small bowl with the remaining Marsala and any leftover steeping juices. Drizzle over the teabread.

Chocolate and sweet potato cake

This might seem an unusual combination, but root vegetables have long been used to add a lovely moist flavour and natural sweetness to sponge cakes.

PREPARATION TIME: 20 minutes, plus cooling

COOKING TIME: 40 minutes

OVEN TEMPERATURE: 160°C (325°F), Gas Mark 3

MAKES 10 slices

250 g (8 oz) sweet potatoes

150 g (5 oz) self-raising flour

25 g (1 oz) cocoa powder

1 teaspoon baking powder

1 teaspoon ground mixed spice

125 g (4 oz) unsalted butter, softened

125 g (4 oz) dark muscovado sugar

1 teaspoon vanilla extract

2 eggs

200 g (7 oz) plain or milk chocolate, chopped

100 g (3½ oz) no-soak prunes, chopped

1 Grease and line the base and sides of a shallow 23 cm (9 inch) square baking tin with greaseproof paper. Grease the paper. Cut the sweet potatoes into 1 cm (½ inch) chunks and cook in boiling water for 10 minutes or until tender. Drain, return to the pan and mash until smooth, then leave to cool.

2 Sift the flour, cocoa powder, baking powder and spice into a mixing bowl. Add the butter, sugar, vanilla extract and eggs and beat for 2 minutes until smooth and creamy. Beat in the mashed sweet potato and half the chocolate.

3 Spread the mixture in the tin and scatter with the remaining chopped chocolate and the prunes. Bake in a preheated oven, 160°C (325°F), Gas Mark 3, for about 30 minutes until just firm. Leave to cool in the tin and serve cut into fingers.

White chocolate and lemongrass cookies *Like many strongly flavoured herbs, lemongrass is delicious in chunky, buttery cookies, especially when combined with chocolate.*

PREPARATION TIME: 15 minutes

COOKING TIME: 15 minutes

OVEN TEMPERATURE: 200°C (400°F), Gas Mark 6

MAKES 16–18

200 g (7 oz) white chocolate, chopped

1 stalk lemongrass

175 g (6 oz) self-raising flour

½ teaspoon baking powder

75 g (3 oz) unsalted butter, diced

50 g (2 oz) sultanas

1 egg, beaten

1 Grease a large baking sheet. Melt 150 g (5 oz) of the chocolate in a small bowl. Bruise the lemongrass by tapping it firmly with a rolling pin. Slice the lemongrass and blend in a food processor until very finely chopped.

2 Add the flour, baking powder and butter and blend until the mixture resembles fine breadcrumbs.

3 Add the melted chocolate, sultanas and egg and blend lightly until the dough binds together. Turn the mixture on to the work surface and shape into a log, about 23 cm (9 inches) long. Cut into chunky slices and place on the baking sheet, spacing the pieces slightly apart and reshaping them if squashed.

4 Bake in a preheated oven, 200°C (400°F), Gas Mark 6, for about 15 minutes until risen and pale golden. Leave on the baking sheet for 2 minutes, then transfer to a wire rack to cool.

5 Melt the remaining chocolate in a small bowl and put in a paper piping bag. Snip off the tip and drizzle the chocolate over the biscuits to decorate.

Chocolate jumble crunches
This no-cook chocolate biscuit is easy to make and reveals a feast of lovely ingredients when it's cut into slices.

PREPARATION TIME: 15 minutes, plus setting

MAKES 24

275 g (9 oz) plain chocolate, broken up
100 g (3½ oz) lightly salted butter
75 g (3 oz) chocolate honeycomb bars
75 g (3 oz) digestive biscuits
50 g (2 oz) walnut pieces
100 g (3½ oz) white chocolate, chopped

1 Melt the plain chocolate and butter in a large mixing bowl and leave to cool. Break the honeycomb bars and biscuits into small pieces.

2 Stir the honeycomb, biscuits and walnuts into the melted chocolate until evenly combined. Scatter the white chocolate into the bowl and fold in gently.

3 Tip the mixture on to a large sheet of nonstick baking paper, spreading it into a log shape about 35 cm (14 inches) long.

4 Bring the paper up over the mixture on the long sides and squeeze the ends of the paper together so that the mixture is compacted into a long sausage shape. Twist the ends of the paper like a sweet wrapper and chill for at least 2 hours or until set.

5 Peel away the paper and cut the log into 1 cm (½ inch) slices. (If the log is too brittle to slice, leave it at room temperature for a while to soften slightly.) Store in a cool place for up to 5 days.

Variation

Use almost any other nuts that you prefer (or have in the cupboard). Hazelnuts, almonds and brazil nuts are all suitable alternatives. You can also try adding raisins, if liked.

White chocolate biscotti
These gorgeous biscuits are baked in one piece, then sliced and re-baked to crisp them up. Serve the Italian way dunked into dessert wine or with some creamy hot chocolate.

PREPARATION TIME: 15 minutes, plus cooling

COOKING TIME: 35 minutes

OVEN TEMPERATURE: 190°C (375°F), Gas Mark 5, then 160°C (325°F), Gas Mark 3

MAKES 24

300 g (10 oz) white chocolate

25 g (1 oz) unsalted butter, softened

225 g (7½ oz) self-raising flour

50 g (2 oz) light muscovado sugar

2 eggs

1 teaspoon vanilla extract

100 g (3½ oz) pecan nuts, roughly chopped

icing sugar, for dusting

1 Lightly grease a large baking sheet. Chop 100 g (3½ oz) of the chocolate into small pieces. Break up the remainder and melt it in a small bowl with the butter. Leave to cool. Sift the flour into a mixing bowl and stir in the sugar, eggs, vanilla extract, nuts and melted chocolate mixture.

2 Add the chopped chocolate and mix to a dough. Tip the mixture on to a lightly floured surface and halve the dough.

3 Shape each half into a log about 25 cm (10 inches) long and flatten to a depth of 2 cm (¾ inch). Space well apart on the baking sheet and bake in a preheated oven, 190°C (375°F), Gas Mark 5, for 18–20 minutes until risen, golden and firm. Remove from the oven and reduce the temperature to 160°C (325°F), Gas Mark 3.

4 Leave the biscuit logs to cool for 20 minutes, then use a serrated knife to slice each length into slices 2 cm (¾ inch) thick. Space them slightly apart on the baking sheet and bake for a further 15 minutes. Dust with icing sugar and transfer to a wire rack to cool.

Thyme, orange and chocolate shortbread

Buttery homemade shortbread is always a real treat, and the subtle additions in this recipe make it even more irresistible.

PREPARATION TIME: 15 minutes, plus chilling

COOKING TIME: 20 minutes

OVEN TEMPERATURE: 180°C (350°F), Gas Mark 4

MAKES 25

1 tablespoon chopped thyme

50 g (2 oz) caster sugar

150 g (5 oz) milk or white chocolate, broken up

250 g (8 oz) plain flour

100 g (3½ oz) rice flour

finely grated rind of 1 orange

200 g (7 oz) lightly salted butter, diced

1 Grease 2 baking sheets. Reserve 1 teaspoon of the chopped thyme. Sprinkle the remainder over 25 g (1 oz) of the sugar on a chopping board and press the thyme into the sugar with the side of the knife. Melt the chocolate in a small bowl.

2 Sift the flour and rice flour into a mixing bowl. Add the reserved thyme, orange rind and butter and rub in with your fingertips until the mixture resembles coarse breadcrumbs.

3 Stir in the remaining sugar and the melted chocolate and mix with a round-bladed knife until the mixture starts to form a dough. Use your hands to bring the mixture together and turn it on to the work surface.

4 Shape into a thick log, about 30 cm (12 inches) long. Roll up in greaseproof paper and chill for 1 hour.

5 Roll the log in the herb sugar. Cut across into thick slices and space slightly apart on the baking sheet. Bake in a preheated oven, 180°C (350°F), Gas Mark 4, for about 20 minutes until beginning to turn pale golden. Transfer to a wire rack to cool.

Thyme, orange and chocolate shortbread

Vanilla-dusted snaps
These are great for dunking into hot chocolate. The shaped dough will keep in the refrigerator if you'd rather cut off slices and serve them freshly baked whenever you fancy.

PREPARATION TIME: 15 minutes, plus chilling

COOKING TIME: 15 minutes

OVEN TEMPERATURE: 180°C (350°F), Gas Mark 4

MAKES 28

150 g (5 oz) plain flour

50 g (2 oz) cocoa powder

½ teaspoon bicarbonate of soda

100 g (3½ oz) light muscovado sugar

100 g (3½ oz) lightly salted butter, softened

1 egg

5 cm (2 inch) vanilla pod

4 tablespoons caster sugar

1 Sift together the flour, cocoa powder and bicarbonate of soda. Put the sugar and butter in a bowl and beat together with an electric whisk until creamy. Add the flour mixture and egg and mix to a dough.

2 Turn the dough on to a lightly floured surface and knead gently until smooth. Shape into a log about 18 cm (7 inches) long. Wrap in clingfilm and chill for at least 30 minutes until firm.

3 Lightly grease 2 large baking sheets. Cut off very thin slices of the log with a sharp knife and space the slices, slightly apart, on the baking sheets. Bake in a preheated oven, 180°C (350°F), Gas Mark 4, for about 15 minutes until slightly risen. If necessary, swap the baking sheets around halfway through cooking.

4 Meanwhile, thinly slice the vanilla pod and blend in a food processor with the sugar until finely ground, removing any bits of the pod that aren't blended. Leave the biscuits on the baking sheets for 2 minutes, transfer to a wire rack and dust with the vanilla sugar. Leave to cool.

Sugar-spiced chocolate twists

Use ready-made puff pastry for these spicy treats and they'll be ready in no time. They are perfect with a cup of creamy cappuccino.

PREPARATION TIME: 15 minutes

COOKING TIME: 15 minutes

OVEN TEMPERATURE: 200°C (400°F), Gas Mark 6

MAKES about 20

1 tablespoon icing sugar, plus plenty for dusting

1½ teaspoons five spice powder

2 tablespoons cocoa powder

350 g (11½ oz) puff pastry, thawed if frozen

100 g (3½ oz) orange-flavoured plain chocolate, broken up

1 Line a large baking sheet with nonstick baking paper. Blend together the icing sugar, the five spice powder and cocoa powder. Roll out the pastry to 40 x 25 cm (16 x 10 inches) on a surface generously dusted with icing sugar and sprinkle half the spiced sugar mixture over half the pastry. Fold the pastry in half and roll again as above. Sprinkle with the remaining spice and sugar and roll out to 38 x 23 cm (15 x 9 inches).

2 Trim off the ragged edges and cut across the pastry to make strips, each about 2 cm (¾ inch) wide. Tie each into a knot and space slightly apart on the baking sheet. Dust generously with icing sugar. Bake in a preheated oven, 200°C (400°F), Gas Mark 6, for about 15 minutes until deep golden and shiny. Transfer to a wire rack to cool.

3 Melt the chocolate in a small bowl and half-dip the biscuits in the chocolate. Transfer to a clean sheet of nonstick baking paper to set.

Crispy chocolate cherry cakes *These are a more exciting version of chocolate cornflake cakes. Make sure you use a cooked, toasted oat cereal rather than one containing raw oats.*

PREPARATION TIME: 15 minutes, plus chilling

MAKES 16–18

375 g (12 oz) toasted oat cereal with fruit and nuts

75 g (3 oz) dried sour cherries, roughly chopped

100 g (3½ oz) plain or milk chocolate, chopped

150 g (5 oz) white chocolate, broken up

1 Line a shallow 23 cm (9 inch) square baking tin with nonstick baking paper. Put the cereal in a large polythene bag and crush it with a rolling pin until coarsely crumbled. Tip it into a bowl and add the cherries and 75 g (3 oz) of the plain or milk chocolate.

2 Melt the white chocolate and add to the cereal, mixing well until evenly combined. Turn into the tin and pack down well with the back of a spoon. Leave in a cool place to set.

3 Melt the remaining chocolate. Use a small teaspoon to scribble lines of melted chocolate diagonally over the mixture. Cut into 16–18 fingers to serve.

Chocolate peanut caramels
The combination of salty peanuts and smooth, sweet chocolate always works well in baking. This moreish mixture is very rich, so cut it into small squares.

PREPARATION TIME: 20 minutes, plus chilling

COOKING TIME: 30 minutes

OVEN TEMPERATURE: 180°C (350°F), Gas Mark 4

MAKES about 25

1 quantity Crisp Chocolate Pastry
(see page 17)

100 g (3½ oz) salted peanuts

200 g (7 oz) golden caster sugar

200 ml (7 fl oz) double cream

50 g (2 oz) unsalted butter

125 g (4 oz) plain chocolate, chopped

1 Roll out the pastry on a lightly floured surface and pack it into the base of a greased shallow 23 cm (9 inch) square baking tin, pressing it down in an even layer. Bake in a preheated oven, 180°C (350°F), Gas Mark 4, for 20 minutes until slightly darker in colour.

2 Blend the peanuts in a food processor or blender until they are ground into small pieces. Put the sugar in a small heavy-based saucepan with 6 tablespoons water. Heat gently until the sugar dissolves, then bring to the boil and boil rapidly for about 5 minutes until the syrup has turned deep golden. Dip the base of the pan straight into cold water to prevent further cooking.

3 Add 100 ml (3½ fl oz) of the cream and the butter and stir over a gentle heat until smooth. Stir in the nuts and leave to thicken for about 15 minutes. Turn the mixture into the pastry-lined tin, spreading it to the edges.

4 Heat the remaining cream in a small pan until almost boiling. Remove from the heat and stir in the chocolate. Leave until melted, stirring frequently until smooth. Tip out over the caramel and spread in an even layer. Chill for at least 2 hours until firm. Serve cut into small squares.

Sweets, treats and drinks *Despite the abundance of shop-bought chocolates available, there's something rather rewarding about making your own, whether to serve after dinner, package up as gifts or simply indulge in while watching a film. This chapter gives recipes for the best Classic Chocolate Truffles, plus a white chocolate variation and some more unusual alternatives. You might even like to make several and serve them as a dessert next time you entertain. The Bite-sized Choc Ices are also great for this purpose.*

Homemade chocolates store well for several days in a very cool place, or in the refrigerator during warm weather if they contain cream. For those that are chocolate-dipped, such as the Chocolate and Pine Nut Praline, make and break up the brittle and store it in an airtight container, ready for chocolate dipping on the day you want to eat it. Rounding off the chapter is a selection of gorgeous chocolate drinks, from a meltingly delicious Chocolate and Coconut Ice to the Sublime Hot Chocolate.

Classic chocolate truffles

These are as good as the absolute best you can buy. They're meltingly smooth and creamy and have the added advantage that you can use your favourite liqueur.

PREPARATION TIME: 20 minutes, plus chilling
MAKES 400 g (13 oz)

150 ml (¼ pint) double cream

250 g (8 oz) plain chocolate, finely chopped

25 g (1 oz) unsalted butter, diced

2 tablespoons liqueur (e.g. brandy, rum, Cointreau or coffee liqueur)

cocoa powder, for dusting

1 Bring the cream just to the boil in a small saucepan. Remove from the heat and tip in the chocolate and butter. Leave until melted, stirring several times until smooth.

2 Turn into a bowl and add the chosen liqueur. Chill for several hours or overnight until firm.

3 Sprinkle plenty of cocoa powder on a large plate. Take a teaspoonful of the chocolate mixture, roll it lightly in the palm of your hand and coat the ball in the cocoa powder. For more rugged, textured-looking truffles, don't roll them, just sprinkle the spoonfuls of chocolate with the cocoa powder.

4 Arrange the truffles in individual paper cases or pile them on a serving dish. Store in a very cool place or in the refrigerator for up to 2 days before serving.

Variations

Add 50 g (2 oz) finely chopped stem ginger or 1 tablespoon ground espresso powder, dissolved in 1 tablespoon boiling water, to the basic mixture before chilling.

White chocolate, saffron and apricot truffles

A hint of saffron and finely chopped apricots give these truffles a slightly sweeter, more aromatic flavour than the classic truffles.

PREPARATION TIME: 25 minutes, plus chilling

MAKES 350 g (11½ oz)

100 ml (3½ fl oz) double cream

generous pinch of saffron threads

200 g (7 oz) white chocolate, finely chopped

50 g (2 oz) no-soak dried apricots, finely chopped

75 g (3 oz) flaked almonds, lightly toasted

icing sugar, for dusting

1 Put the cream in a small saucepan and crumble in the saffron. Bring slowly to the boil and remove from the heat.

2 Add the chocolate to the cream and leave until melted, stirring frequently until smooth. Turn the mixture into a bowl and stir in the apricots. Chill for several hours or overnight until firm.

3 Crush the almonds into small flakes and scatter on a plate. Take a teaspoonful of the chocolate mixture, form it into a ball between the palms of your hands and roll in the almonds. Dust with icing sugar. Repeat with the remaining mixture. Store in a very cool place or in the refrigerator for up to 2 days before serving.

Variation

Roll the truffles in 75 g (3 oz) skinned and chopped pistachio nuts instead of almonds.

Fruit and nut discs
Use a small biscuit cutter to make neat rounds of these chocolates. The chocolate trimmings, if not nibbled away, can be stored and re-melted in another recipe.

PREPARATION TIME: 10 minutes, plus setting

MAKES 18

100 g (3½ oz) **plain chocolate, broken up**

100 g (3½ oz) **milk chocolate, broken up**

100 g (3½ oz) **white chocolate, broken up**

125 g (4 oz) **dried tropical fruit medley (e.g. pineapple, mango, papaya, melon)**

25 g (1 oz) **blanched almonds**

25 g (1 oz) **unblanched hazelnuts**

1 Melt all the chocolate in separate bowls. Spoon on to 3 separate sheets of nonstick baking paper and spread to 16 x 12 cm (6½ x 5 inch) rectangles.

2 Use a 5 cm (2 inch) round metal cutter to make 6 impressions in each chocolate rectangle to mark the edges of each disc.

3 Cut the dried fruits into small, flattish pieces and arrange them within the marked discs along with the nuts. Chill or leave in a cool place until the chocolate is set but not brittle.

4 Use the cutter to cut out the discs and carefully lift them from the paper. Store in a cool place.

Bite-sized choc ices
Serve these as a delicious accompaniment to after-dinner coffee on a warm summer's evening. They can be made up to a month ahead, so there's no last-minute preparation involved.

PREPARATION TIME: 40 minutes, plus freezing

MAKES about 30

750 ml (1¼ pints) vanilla-, chocolate- or coffee-flavoured ice cream, thoroughly frozen

200 g (7 oz) plain chocolate, chopped

200 g (7 oz) milk chocolate, chopped

25 g (1 oz) finely chopped hazelnuts, lightly toasted

1 Line a large baking sheet with nonstick baking paper and freeze for 15 minutes. Pour boiling water into a small bowl, then use a melon baller to scoop balls of the ice cream and place them on the baking sheet, dipping the melon baller in the water and wiping it dry each time. (You'll need to work fairly quickly before the ice cream melts. If it does, pop everything back in the freezer until it's firm again, then carry on).

2 Once you've scooped as many balls as possible, pack the ice cream down again until solid and re-freeze it so that you can make more scoops later. Freeze the ice cream scoops for at least 2 hours.

3 Melt the chocolate in separate bowls. Push a wooden cocktail stick into each ice cream. Use a dessertspoon to coat them, one at a time, with plain or milk chocolate, scattering each with a few chopped nuts as you go. Return to the freezer until ready to serve. If you want to freeze the choc ices for a long time, transfer them to a rigid container, covered with a lid or foil.

Chocolate dates with pistachios
These are lovely with after-dinner coffee or as a present for someone who isn't too keen on the sweeter chocolate treats.

PREPARATION TIME: 25 minutes, plus setting

MAKES 18

50 g (2 oz) shelled pistachio nuts

15 g (½ oz) icing sugar

15 g (½ oz) caster sugar

1 tablespoon orange liqueur

18 Medjool dates

100 g (3½ oz) plain or orange-flavoured plain chocolate, broken up

1 Put the pistachios in a small bowl and cover with boiling water. Leave for 1 minute, then drain. Rub firmly between several thicknesses of kitchen paper to remove the skins.

2 Put the pistachios in a food processor and blend until fairly finely ground. Add the sugars and liqueur and blend to a thick paste. Turn on to the work surface and shape into a thin log. Cut into 18 evenly sized pieces.

3 Cut a slit across the top of each date and remove the stone. Tuck a piece of the pistachio paste in the centre.

4 Melt the chocolate in a small bowl. Half-dip the stuffed dates in the chocolate and transfer to a sheet of nonstick baking paper. Leave to set in a very cool place or in the refrigerator for about 1 hour.

Sweet chocolate sushi

This is a stunning variation on the familiar savoury sushi. It's fun to make and a great after-dinner treat, particularly for those who prefer less-sweet chocolate flavours.

PREPARATION TIME: 40 minutes, plus chilling
COOKING TIME: 10 minutes
MAKES 25–30

1 kiwifruit, skinned

½ small mango, skinned

3 tablespoons tequila or vodka

250 g (8 oz) Japanese sushi rice

400 ml (14 fl oz) can coconut milk

100 g (3½ oz) caster sugar

1 tablespoon white wine vinegar

100 g (3½ oz) plain chocolate, broken up

1 Cut the fruits into 5 mm (¼ inch) thick sticks and mix them with the liqueur. Put the rice in a heavy-based saucepan with the coconut milk. Bring to the boil, then simmer very gently for 10 minutes, stirring frequently, until the rice has the consistency of a thick risotto. Add the sugar and vinegar, cover and leave to cool.

2 Melt the chocolate. Draw 3 rectangles, each 24 x 10 cm (9½ x 4 inches), on 3 sheets of nonstick baking paper so that one long side is on the edge of the paper. Spread the chocolate over them.

3 Spoon the cooled rice on to 3 separate sheets of paper, spreading each to 24 x 8 cm (9½ x 3¼ inches) and pressing down very firmly with the back of a wetted spoon. Arrange a thin line of fruit down the centre of each, reserving the juices.

4 Carefully roll up the fruits and rice in the paper, squeezing the edges of the paper tightly together so that the rice is tightly packed. Roll up the rice in the chocolate. (The chocolate edges should just meet.) Chill for 2 hours then remove the paper.

5 Use a serrated knife to cut the sushi into logs. Drizzle with the reserved juices.

Sweet chocolate sushi

Creamy mint-choc fudge
There's no thermometer or sugar boiling to worry about with this creamy, melt-in-the-mouth fudge recipe. Use the very best chocolate for rich and delicious results.

PREPARATION TIME: 15 minutes, plus chilling
MAKES 800 g (1 lb 12 oz)

40 g (1½ oz) strong peppermints
500 g (1 lb) plain chocolate, chopped
400 g (13 oz) can sweetened condensed milk
50 g (2 oz) milk or white chocolate, melted

1 Put the peppermints in a polythene bag and crush with a rolling pin until broken into small pieces. Continue to roll and flatten the mints until ground to a powder. Line a shallow 18 cm (7 inch) baking tin with nonstick baking paper.

2 Put the plain chocolate and condensed milk in a heatproof bowl over a pan of gently simmering water. Leave until melted, stirring frequently. Stir in the ground peppermints.

3 Beat the mixture until the ingredients are combined and turn it into the tin, spreading it into the corners. Level the surface and leave to cool. Chill for at least 2 hours.

4 Lift the fudge out of the tin and peel away the paper from around the sides. Melt the milk or white chocolate and put it in a paper piping bag. Snip off the tip and scribble lines of chocolate over the fudge. Cut into 2 cm (¾ inch) squares and transfer to a serving plate.

Variation
Omit the mints and add the finely grated rind of 1 small orange and 1 teaspoon instant espresso powder.

Chocolate and pine nut praline

The secret of success is to get the caramel to the right colour – a deep golden-brown. If you overcook it, the resulting praline will taste bitter.

PREPARATION TIME: 15 minutes, plus setting

COOKING TIME: 10 minutes

MAKES 225 g (7½ oz)

50 g (2 oz) pine nuts

25 g (1 oz) flaked almonds

200 g (7 oz) caster sugar

50 g (2 oz) plain chocolate, broken up

1 Lightly toast the pine nuts and almonds. Blend in a food processor until the nuts are broken into slightly smaller pieces, but not too finely ground. Lightly oil a large, clean baking sheet.

2 Put the sugar and 5 tablespoons of water in a small heavy-based saucepan and heat very gently, stirring until the sugar dissolves. Bring to the boil and cook, without stirring until the syrup has turned to golden caramel. This will take 6–8 minutes. Immediately dip the base of the pan in cold water to prevent further cooking and stir in the nuts.

3 Working quickly, turn the praline on to the baking sheet, spreading it out in a thin layer before it starts to set. Leave for about an hour until brittle.

4 Melt the chocolate in a small bowl. Line a baking sheet with greaseproof paper. Break the praline into jagged pieces and half-dip them in the melted chocolate, transferring them to the paper as you work. Leave to set.

White chocolate and mango milkshake *Like all the best milkshakes, this is thick, creamy and ice cool, perfect for enjoying during a heat wave.*

PREPARATION TIME: 10 minutes, plus chilling
COOKING TIME: 5 minutes
SERVES 2

150 g (5 oz) white chocolate, finely chopped
250 ml (8 fl oz) milk
2 ripe mangoes, chilled
2 scoops vanilla ice cream
chocolate curls, to decorate (see page 6)

1 Put 100 g (3½ oz) of the chocolate in a small saucepan with 100 ml (3½ fl oz) of the milk and heat gently, stirring frequently, until the chocolate has melted. Pour into a bowl and leave to cool.

2 Melt the remaining chocolate. Use a teaspoon to swirl the chocolate around the insides of 2 300 ml (½ pint) clear glasses, working from the base to the top of the glasses in a spiral pattern. (Don't worry about keeping the spiral neat – it'll look effective no matter how uneven it is.) Chill while making the milkshake.

3 Halve and stone the mangoes. Cut away the skins and chop the flesh into a food processor. Blend to a smooth purée, scraping any pieces down from the sides of the bowl. Add the chocolate milk, remaining milk and ice cream and blend until smooth.

4 Pour the milkshake into the glasses and serve sprinkled with chocolate curls.

White chocolate and mango milkshake

Chocolate and coconut ice
This cooling blend falls somewhere between a milkshake and a melting sorbet, almost drinkable through a straw but easier to enjoy with a long spoon.

PREPARATION TIME: 10 minutes, plus freezing
COOKING TIME: 5 minutes
SERVES 4

750 ml (1¼ pints) milk
100 g (3½ oz) creamed coconut, chopped
25 g (1 oz) cocoa powder
100 g (3½ oz) caster sugar
100 g (3½ oz) plain chocolate, chopped

1 Put 250 ml (8 fl oz) of the milk in a medium-sized saucepan with the coconut, cocoa powder and sugar and heat gently until the coconut and sugar have dissolved. Bring to the boil and boil for 3 minutes.

2 Remove from the heat and tip in the chocolate. Leave until the chocolate has melted, stirring frequently. Leave to cool.

3 Pour into a shallow freezer container with the remaining milk and freeze for 4–6 hours until frozen around the edges but still slightly slushy in the centre. Turn into a food processor and blend lightly until evenly slushy. Serve immediately or return to the freezer for another time.

Cinnamon lassi

A drink fit for almost any time of day, from a leisurely breakfast through to a late-afternoon cooler. Any extra keeps well in the refrigerator overnight.

PREPARATION TIME: 2 minutes, plus chilling

COOKING TIME: 2 minutes

SERVES 2

200 ml (7 fl oz) milk

½ teaspoon ground cinnamon

75 g (3 oz) plain chocolate, broken up

200 g (7 oz) natural yogurt

3 tablespoons vanilla syrup

2 long cinnamon sticks

chocolate curls, to decorate (see page 6)

1 Put half the milk in a small saucepan with the cinnamon. Bring just to the boil, then remove it from the heat and stir in the chocolate. Leave until melted, stirring frequently.

2 Stir in the remaining milk and the yogurt and vanilla syrup and whisk until frothy with either a balloon or immersion whisk.

3 Pour into glasses and add a cinnamon stick to each. Serve scattered with chocolate curls.

Chocolate martinis

If you have a cocktail shaker, use it to mix the drink with plenty of crushed ice. If not, make it a couple of hours in advance so that it has time to chill.

PREPARATION TIME: 5 minutes, plus chilling

SERVES 4

plenty of cocoa powder, for dusting
100 ml (3½ fl oz) gin, plus 1 tablespoon
40 g (1½ oz) plain chocolate, broken up
200 ml (7 fl oz) dry vermouth

1 Sprinkle plenty of cocoa powder on a plate. Use your finger to moisten the rims of 4 cocktail glasses with the tablespoon of gin. Immediately dip each rim in the cocoa powder to coat in a thin band.

2 Melt the chocolate with the remaining gin, stirring frequently, until the mixture is smooth. Stir in the vermouth.

3 Shake the mixture in a cocktail shaker with ice, or chill for at least 2 hours, before serving.

Sublime hot chocolate
Proper hot chocolate is always made with a pure blend of good quality chocolate and milk. The creamy topping is a delicious indulgence but not absolutely vital.

PREPARATION TIME: 3 minutes

COOKING TIME: 3 minutes

SERVES 2

100 g (3½ oz) plain chocolate, broken up

350 ml (12 fl oz) milk

100 ml (3½ fl oz) whipping cream, lightly whipped

grated chocolate, to sprinkle

1 Melt the chocolate in a small bowl. Heat the milk in a small pan until hot but not boiling. Stir a little of the hot milk into the melted chocolate, scraping up the chocolate from around the sides of the bowl, then pour the chocolate milk into the milk pan.

2 Whisk together and pour into large mugs or heatproof glasses. Spoon over the cream and sprinkle with grated chocolate.

Variation

For a sweeter flavour, use a good quality milk chocolate.

Irish chocolate coffee
Smooth, comforting and with a warming smack of whiskey, this creamy chocolate coffee is the perfect tipple to relax with.

PREPARATION TIME: 5 minutes

COOKING TIME: 2 minutes

SERVES 2

1 small orange

15 g (½ oz) caster sugar

25 g (1 oz) plain chocolate, chopped

2 tablespoons Irish whiskey

300 ml (½ pint) freshly made strong black coffee

100 ml (3½ fl oz) whipping cream

1 Pare 2 long strips of orange rind and put them in a medium-sized saucepan with the sugar and 125 ml (4 fl oz) water. Heat gently until the sugar dissolves, then bring to the boil. Remove from the heat and stir in the chocolate until melted.

2 Remove the orange strips and add the whiskey and coffee. Pour into 2 tall heatproof glasses.

3 Lightly whip the cream with 2 tablespoons orange juice and spoon over the coffee. Serve immediately.

Chocolate velvet with tuilles

This is a fabulously smooth, chocolaty version of an espresso, served in small cups because it's so rich. The chocolate tuilles are perfect for dipping, so make plenty.

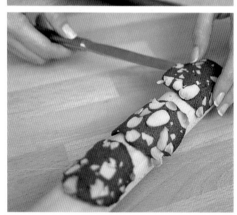

PREPARATION TIME: 20 minutes

COOKING TIME: 20 minutes

OVEN TEMPERATURE: 220°C (425°F), Gas Mark 7

MAKES 4 espressos and 20 biscuits

25 g (1 oz) flaked almonds

1 egg white

50 g (2 oz) light muscovado sugar

1 tablespoon plain flour

2 tablespoons cocoa powder

2 tablespoons double cream

25 g (1 oz) lightly salted butter, melted

300 ml (½ pint) freshly made espresso coffee

75 g (3 oz) plain chocolate, finely chopped

1 teaspoon dark muscovado sugar

1 To make the tuilles, line a baking sheet with nonstick baking paper. Lightly crush the almonds to break them into smaller pieces. Whisk together the egg white and light muscovado sugar, then add the flour, cocoa powder, cream and butter, beating to a smooth paste.

2 Put 4 teaspoonfuls of the mixture, spaced well apart, on the baking sheet and spread slightly with the back of the spoon. Scatter with a few almonds and bake in a preheated oven, 220°C (425°F), Gas Mark 7, for 4–5 minutes until the edges darken.

3 Remove from the oven and carefully lift the tuilles over a rolling pin so that they set in a curved shape. Transfer to a wire rack to cool, and make the remainder of the tuilles in the same way.

4 Pour the espresso into a small pan and add the chocolate and dark muscovado sugar. Heat very gently, stirring frequently, until the chocolate has melted. Use an electric or hand whisk to froth up the mixture. Pour into tiny cups and serve immediately with the chocolate tuilles.

Index

Acknowledgments

Photography: © Octopus Publishing Group Ltd / Stephen Conroy

Executive Editor Sarah Ford
Editor Charlotte Wilson
Executive Art Editor and Design Joanna MacGregor
Production Controller Manjit Sihra
Food Stylist Joanna Farrow